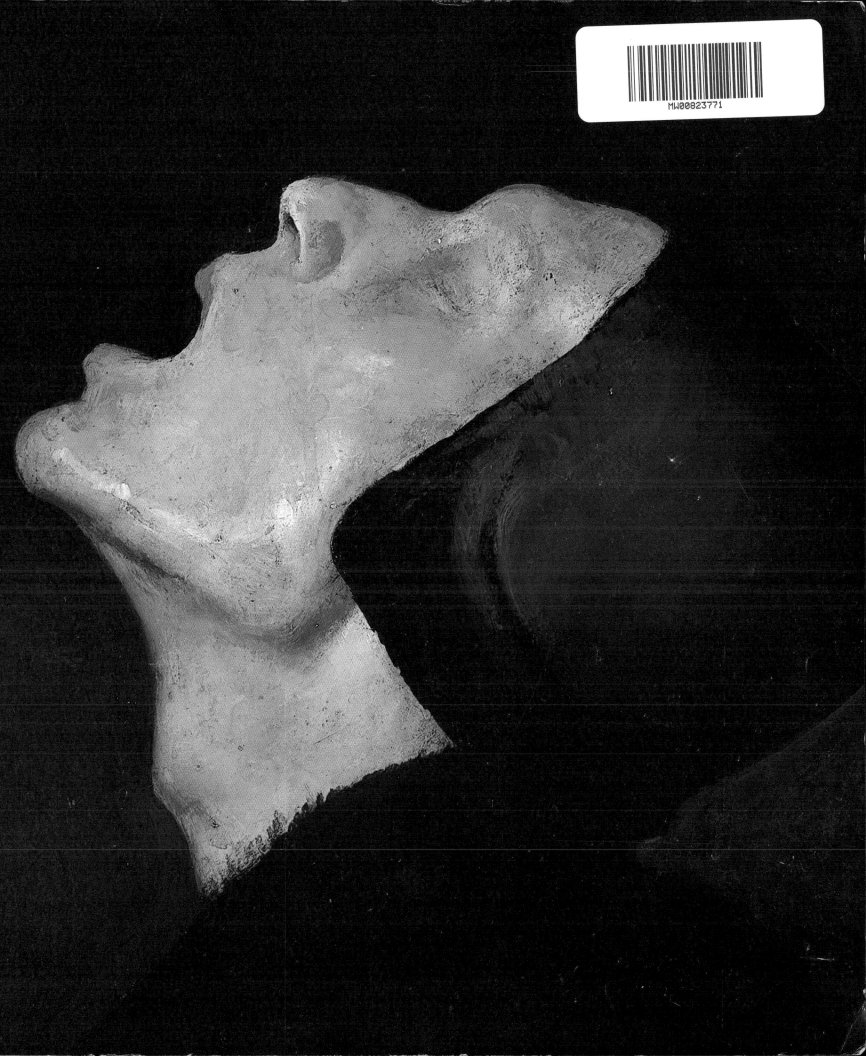

MW00823771

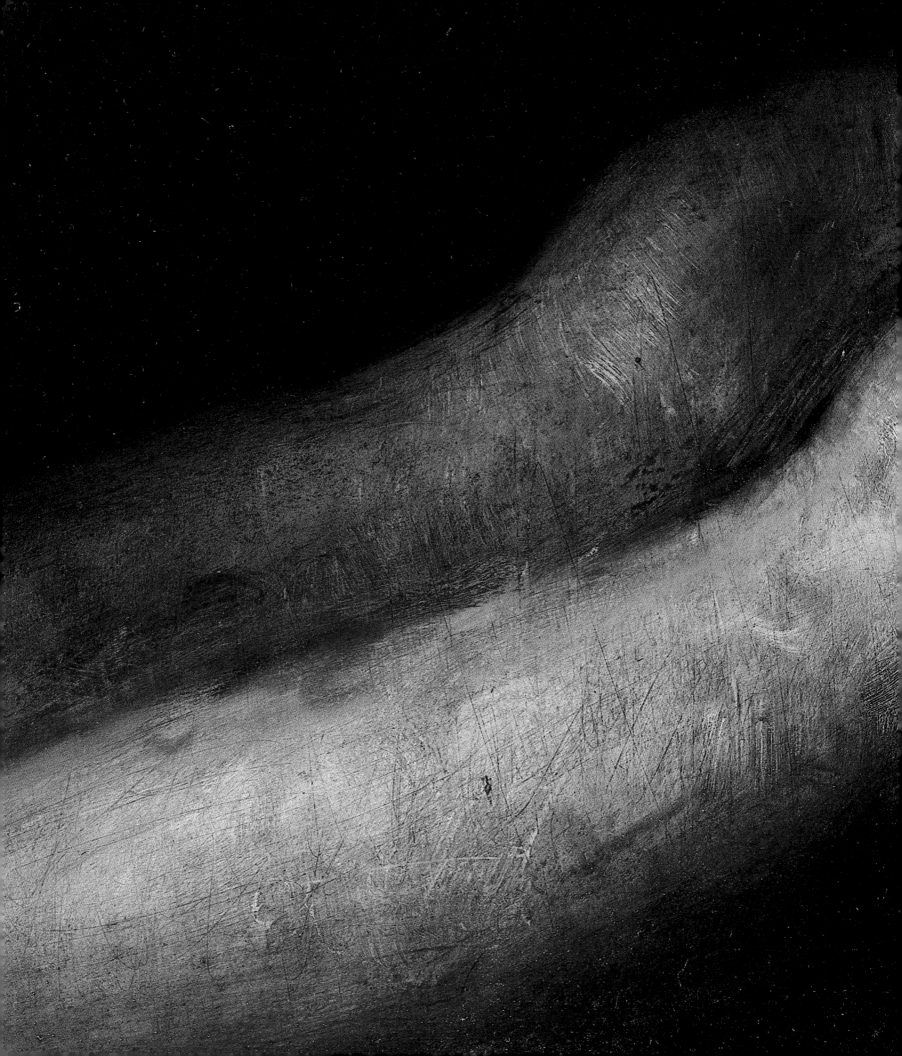

# ODD NERDRUM

Jan Åke Pettersson

# ODD NERDRUM
## STORYTELLER AND SELF-REVEALER

Astrup Fearnley Museet for Moderne Kunst
Astrup Fearnley Museum of Modern Art

ASCHEHOUG

# CONTENTS

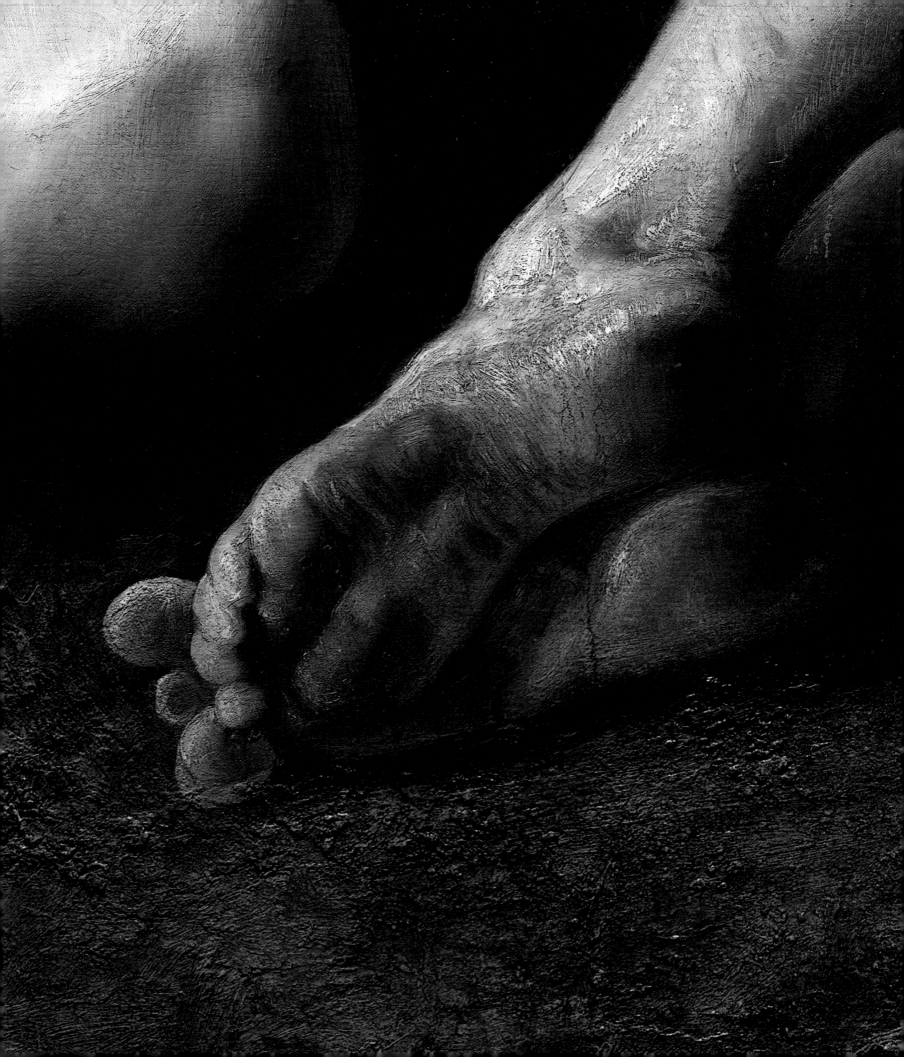

# PREFACE

THIS BOOK IS PUBLISHED ON THE OCCASION OF THE FALL 1998
exhibition of works by Odd Nerdrum at the Astrup Fearnley Museum
of Modern Art in Oslo and at Kunsthal Rotterdam in the Nether-
lands. Instead of a catalogue commenting on the works exhibited, this
book contains a much broader presentation of the artist and his work.
Some readers may recognize my approach to his work from my first
book on the artist, published in 1988. Like then, my goal has been to
contribute to an understanding of Nerdrum's pictures by penetrating
and conveying some of what the artist himself wants to express
through them – that which might be his intentions. Those who find
an artist's statements and self-assessments harmful to their own experience of his work may want to refrain from reading this text. Those
who choose to have a guided tour into the world of Odd Nerdrum are
still free to arrive at their own understanding of his paintings. Any interpretation of statements, whether they are in the form of words or
images, can never be true or false. At best they are only more or less
likely. Yet I hope the reader will find the text of interest, for I believe
it reveals a new dimension in Odd Nerdrum's work, which to an even
greater extent than in any previous analysis relies on autobiographical
elements.

In my work to make the text more readable and less cryptic, I am
indebted to the Museum's director, Hans-Jacob Brun, and its curator,
Øystein Ustvedt, for their comments. Thanks are also extended to Per
Lundgren, Torill Mobech-Hanssen, David Sandved, and Tove
Storsveen at Aschehoug.

The exhibition of Odd Nerdrum's paintings is made possible
through contributions by Astrup Fearnley A/S and The Thomas
Fearnley, Heddy and Nils Astrup Foundation. In the process of com-
piling it, I have had the pleasure of assisting the museum's curator,
Øystein Ustvedt. On behalf of both of us I convey our gratitude to
Bjørn Rønneberg on the board of the Museum, as well as to Forum
Gallery, New York, for their kind assistance. And, not least, to Odd
Nerdrum himself, for having made both the exhibition and the book
possible. Finally, on behalf of the Astrup Fearnley Museum of
Modern Art, I want to extend our most sincere thanks to all the
museums and private collectors in Europe and the United States
who have so generously lent their paintings to the exhibitions.

*Oslo, May 1998*
Jan Åke Pettersson

# OLD MASTER IDEALS

ENTERING THE LOBBY OF THE NATIONAL GALLERY in Oslo on Friday, 13 August 1993, on a casual visit, I saw Odd Nerdrum descending the stairs from the upper floor. He stopped and beckoned me over to join him, looking unusually excited. In his hand was a large envelope, and without further introduction he pulled a couple of photographs from it and asked me to study them. They showed a youngish man, but appeared themselves to be somewhat dated. In an attempt to confirm my immediate hunch I reached for Nerdrum's large head of gray hair and pushed it back to compare the hairline. He met my questioning eyes and nodded: «Yes, I believe it is my father, my real father.» Odd Nerdrum was then forty-nine years old. Ever since childhood he had had a strong feeling that something was not quite right in his relationship with the father who raised him – the lawyer and managing director of the Norwegian division of the Scandinavian Airlines System, Johan Nerdrum. This had troubled him all along, especially in adolescence. No one ever told him that he had any grounds for this strong discomfort, and yet the feeling of being an outsider and not belonging was always there.[1] It was only when Johan Nerdrum died, in 1991, and Odd received word that he was not wanted at the funeral, that his suspicions were confirmed.

The following summer new information came to light. A pupil of his, Stig Ristesund, told him about an elderly architect he had noticed on a visit to his home town, Haugesund, on the west coast. Ristesund had happened to be standing in front of him while he gave a public presentation of his new building on the grounds of the town's Rudolf Steiner school. Everything about this man reminded the pupil of Odd Nerdrum – the same eyes, the same manners, and the same slightly nervous twitches.[2] The architect's name was David Sandved, and, in addition to having designed several major buildings in town, among them the art museum, he was a well-known anthroposophist and a respected intellectual in his community. Nerdrum recalled how he, at seventeen, had borrowed a book from his mother carrying the dedication: «To Lillemor from David.» At the time he had been told that

David had been his mother's boyfriend. He now confronted her with the new piece of information. Her immediate response was to admit to the fact, but the following day she retracted it. Nerdrum put the matter aside until the summer of 1993, at which point he could wait no longer. He called Ristesund in Haugesund and asked him to use his contacts at the local newspaper to get hold of some photographs of Sandved. Two months after he had shown me those photographs at the National Gallery, he visited the now eighty-one-year-old architect. The final confirmation of his parentage came as an enormous relief. Not only was his biological father a man he could respect and identify with – the encounter made the pieces in the puzzle of his own life begin to fall into place.

The year of the reunion he painted *A Father Finding His Son* (1). Instead of depicting the event as it happened, Nerdrum placed himself in the passive role, allowing the motif to express his long-standing yearning for a father. In this version it is the son who is found, asleep in a strained and contorted position. He is surrounded by the attributes of the restless wanderer. The father finally appears, delivering him of the anxiety and the pain. United they drift free from the discomforts of life, returning to the conciliatory twilight land across the sea, where the father had come from. Odd Nerdrum had for years had the idea that the solution to his longing for a father would in some way be related to the sea. In 1978, when he himself was about to become a father, this idea materialized in the children's book *Havfuglen* [The Seabird]. The setting is a small coastal community in the north of Norway. In several of the illustrations, painted that summer at Skutvik, the ocean and the beach play a central role (2,3). The story is explicitly autobiographical, only nominally camouflaged in the author's choice of a main character, the little girl Eline, whom we follow from the age of six into her early teens. Nerdrum seems to have understood far more than he knew at the time. For, like himself, the little girl had been born a love child, and spent years in uncertainty of her father's identity and destiny.

In the book Nerdrum describes Eline's absent mother,

occupied with work or with her spare-time pursuit of local males. Eline is left on her own as a friendless outcast in the community. Having come across a photograph of her father when she was left alone one night, she sees him in a dream. He is a sailor and will soon return with his ship to fetch her. Enchanted by this dream she spends days sitting on a rock by the shore, watching the sea. Soon she is joined by the youngest and the oldest members of the community, who now want to share her mystical preoccupation. They all watch and wait, but only Eline knows what they are waiting for. One day a shipwreck appears out of the fog, surrendered by the polar ice after centuries consigned to oblivion. Eline makes her way onboard and finds the body of the man she believes to be her father. He is wearing the clothes of times past and has a scar above one eye. She touches him and catches a fever, her skin turning a yellowish color, and soon she dies. In this story Nerdrum had not simply included his longing for the return of a father. The tale also represented his longing for the vanished splendor and beauty of the great art of the past. The name of the once powerful, iced-in ship was *Ercole*, named after the Italian port where the baroque painter Caravaggio finally collapsed from a fever in the summer of 1610, follow-

ing a four-year flight from Roman authorities. Onboard the vessel were also Nerdrum's artistic «Fathers» – the old masters, his «dead friends» – an enticing, but apparently also dangerous matter.

In the summer of 1943, when she met and resumed her affair with David Sandved, Lillemor Nerdrum had been married for a few years and was well settled in her husband's home town of Tønsberg. The lawyer Johan Nerdrum was a leading figure in the Norwegian resistance movement during the war, and in its later stages he was sent to Stockholm to direct the military operations from there. A couple of weeks before his wife was to give birth, she was smuggled out of Norway to the town of Helsingborg in southern Sweden; and this is where she gave birth to Odd Olav on 8 April 1944. A few weeks later she was able to join her husband in Stockholm, where they remained until the end of the war.

This year in exile from Hitler's shadow was the start of a difficult childhood for Nerdrum. When he was only a couple of years old, his mother left to study for several months at the Fashion Academy in New York, in order to be able to open a dressmaker's shop on her return to Oslo. The boy was sent to an orphanage – «like a dog to a kennel,» as he put it later when recalling his early childhood: «As I was growing up, I had a strong feeling that they wanted to get rid of me, a feeling of being unwanted.»[3]

The divorce that separated him from the father figure of Johan Nerdrum, and his side of the family, happened when he was about six. Having a mother who spent much of her time in the shop, and being responsible for a brother three years younger, left the boy with too many worries to be able to adjust to the demands for obedience placed on him when he was enrolled in school a year too early. So his mother delayed his starting school until the fall of 1951. She was then foresighted enough to place him at the Rudolf Steiner school in Oslo, where the nationally famous author Jens Bjørneboe became his teacher. Things improved considerably for the boy under the care of this righteous anarchist and inspired anthroposophist. In his year-end reports every year until 1957 Bjørneboe painted a pretty vivid picture of his student's character and development. In his first report he described the boy as «a sensitive and most exceptional child. At times his idiosyncrasy makes itself felt to the point of hampering him in establishing relationships

2. *The Seabird*, 1978. Oil on wood, 10 ½ x 14 ½ in.
3. *Old People and Children by the Sea*, 1978. Oil on wood, 10 ¼ x 17 ¼ in.

1. *A Father Finding his Son,* 1993. Oil on canvas, 63 x 63 in.

with the other children in the class. Odd often imposes a very strict discipline on himself and finds it difficult to understand that not everyone can manage to do the same. It may be tempting to see this as a kind of recalcitrance, a form of self-centeredness, but all his eccentricity appears to be rooted in the deeper layers of his soul. One would do well to overlook a considerable extent of peculiarity on his part.»

His stepfather found it difficult to accept the boy's eccentricity and individuality. Following the divorce they saw each other only infrequently, but throughout the fifties the father tried repeatedly to involve the boy in sports or other group activities, for him to be like other children, but with little success. Odd preferred to draw, paint, or to look at art books. Bjørneboe had also noticed that he was highly gifted musically, but he never got a piano, and he detested popular music. Ski trips in the winter and sailing in the summer were to him only obligations to be avoided whenever possible. He did not mind being in nature or hovering above it in the armada of airplanes that Johan Nerdrum now commanded. His preference was to listen to his stepfather reading from the classic fairytales. And when left to his own devices, he enjoyed illustrating them on paper. When, at the age of seven, he announced that he would like to be «a painter, when grown up,» there was not much encouragement. Bjørneboe, who had quoted this in his first student report, and who was himself a trained artist, from the very beginning saw Nerdrum as highly talented: «Already that fall (1951) his drawing showed great improvement, also becoming unusually distinctive. For the rest of the school year he has been one of the top students in his drawing and painting class, which is saying a lot . . . I believe not one of my teaching colleagues has ever seen children's drawings as peculiar as those made by Odd during the school year.»

Throughout the fifties Bjørneboe continued to record his observations of «this noble, and thoroughly artistic being, original, independent, and highly competent in all his efforts,» and in 1954 he notes that «he no longer seems 'special' except in a most positive sense.» In the summer of 1957 he ends his last report by stating that: «Odd may be the most exceptional and original student I have ever had. He is highly gifted artistically and has a uniquely noble disposition. He is in many ways a loner, but thanks to his keen and broad interests he still makes friends easily. Anything Odd does carries the strong and unmistakable mark of his personality. Along with his great – at times disturbingly great – sensibility he has a sound, discerning intellect.» And, he adds, seemingly at the thought of what may lie ahead for such an individual: «Odd comes into his own only where his nature is met with respect and understanding.»

A few more years would pass before he subjected his surroundings to any greater artistic challenges. Expressionism had taken hold of him at about seventeen, following his exposure to Johan Nerdrum's collection of modern Norwegian art and all the gallery visits he made in the company of his uncle Michael Clauson. In 1962, when he made his artistic début at Unge Kunstneres Samfund [The society of young artists], he did so with woodcuts clearly inspired by Georges Rouault. That fall he had entered the National Academy of Art in Oslo, and it was in this connection that he began having serious doubts concerning the art of our century. The application had included three paintings. Two of them were reasonably finished, while the third one had been hurriedly thrown together to meet the deadline. The fact that this was the one that the committee found so promising as to admit him into the nation's leading art school, made him question the criteria applied to modern art. This was too easy; it offered too little resistance. Was he entering a sinking ship?

The answer came at Moderna Museet in Stockholm, during a visit in the late fall of 1962 with his fellow students. Nerdrum was not unfamiliar with the latest trends in contemporary art. The previous couple of years he had visited the library at the American embassy regularly to read their art magazines, and earlier in the year he had visited the Museum of Modern Art in New York, while working as a sailor during the summer. It therefore came as no great revelation to him when he was confronted with Moderna Museet's recent acquisition of the neo-dadaist Robert Rauschenberg: a stuffed, painted goat wearing a car tire, placed on a collage of scrap wood and photocopies. Looking back on his reaction at that time, he describes his disappointment: «Modernism felt old and sad. I had seen so much of it that I was fed up.»[4] To Nerdrum the stuffed goat came to signify modern art's inability to convey what he considered to be important human values.

The rebellious power of the avant-garde movements at the beginning of the century had now been reduced to a new kind of conventional salon art. In it he found only emptiness and artistic self-annihilation. By means of irony – overused already in the fifties – contemporary artists had removed themselves from all that he saw as genuine, but not from the veneer of the commercial society they dealt with. Instead they were its true heirs, a heritage Nerdrum rejected. The ship he had boarded had already sunk, and a few years later, when he was able to speak through the media, his message was clear: «There appears to be a wave of senility and apathy swamping the art scene . . . The painter is left empty when dealing with life. He has lost touch with the functional within himself and in nature.»[5] Odd Nerdrum had turned anti-modernist.

Stockholm also offered him an alternative. Only a few hundred yards away from Moderna Museet was Nationalmuseum, which he visited afterwards together with his fellow students. After a while he found himself alone, spellbound before Rembrandt's large history painting of the Dutch Batavians pledging allegiance to their leader Claudius Civilis before rebelling against the Romans (fig.). He was captivated by the painting, and most of his remai-

ning time in Stockholm was spent in front of it. He soon realized that he had found the love of his life. Then and there he made his decision to follow in the footsteps of the old masters. In Rembrandt's glowing tenebrism and portentous solemnity he rediscovered not only all the basic and timelessly human qualities that he felt had been left behind in contemporary art. He also recognized a natural and physically functioning world apparently consistent with the greatest well-being, when he later described his experience of Rembrandt as how «it was like entering the privy of my childhood, lifting the lid, looking straight down into the darkness.»[6]

An already keen interest in classical art had prepared him for this encounter. He had seen Rembrandt and the other old masters many times, most recently at the Metropolitan in New York that same summer. His fascination with this kind of art had, however, started at eleven, when he got hold of a book on Botticelli. The sight of Botticelli's beautiful, melancholy faces comforted him, and he is still convinced that all those evenings spent in the company of this early Renaissance painter continue to leave their mark on his own compositions. He made frequent visits to the National Gallery, particularly to study the early work of

Rembrandt: *The Batavian's Oath to Claudius Civilis*, 1661. Nationalmuseum, Stockholm.

Edvard Munch. And before his thirteenth birthday he had already twice hung the airline pass around his neck to make day trips on his own to Copenhagen. There he took the bus to the collections of Egyptian and Greco-Roman sculpture in the Glyptotek, concluding his excursions with a look at the paintings in the Danish national museum of art. One incident he recalls as having made a great impression on him in his encounters with books on art history happened when he was about fifteen. He was lying in bed studying Goya's *Saturn* (fig.): «I was surprised to see that it had been painted such a long time ago. It seemed more modern than any other picture I had seen. That is when I understood why Munch's *Scream* had been made and why Francis Bacon's paintings look the way they do. I was un-

der the impression that it was something new, but now realized that Goya had covered the entire range in this form of expression, that this was far more powerful and terrifying than anything done since . . . Looking at Goya's work, you can see that there is blood running through his veins.»[7]

Another reason for Nerdrum's preference for the dusky world of the old masters can be found in his search for a father figure. The relationship to his legal father became even more strained after his remarriage when Odd was eleven. All through his childhood he had sought refuge in the grandfather whose name he carried, Odd Nerdrum. A former member of the national assembly, with his own law office in Tønsberg, he was an educated and sophisticated man. But above all he was kindly inclined to the exceptional and inquisitive youth who often came to visit him and to discuss art, music, and literature. Behind the heavy draperies and massive antiques in his grandfather's old-fashioned, respectable upper-class home, the boy found security and spiritual nourishment, and, above all, what he calls «a central father figure when growing up.»[8] Thus Nerdrum's choice was as much a protest against the cold and rejecting modernism of his parents' generation as it was an expression of his need to recreate the safe and encouraging atmosphere of his grandfather's protective world. However, he also identified with the one-eyed rebel Claudius Civilis, who, sword in hand, waged war against a clearly mightier opponent. Soon Nerdrum's self-image would include the picture of himself as a rebel in a blind world of art, where even a «one-eyed» outsider could make his way with his brush and emerge as a king.

Back at the Academy Nerdrum embarked on the most radical artistic project in post-war art, confirming to everyone the independence and originality Bjørneboe had seen in him. His rejection of the established rules of modernism was both unheard of and incomprehensible on the Norwegian art scene, where it was still a challenge to gain acceptance for the latest international trends. In the spring of 1964, when he participated in a group exhibition at Kunstnerforbundet [The artist's association], for the first time showing his «old-masterly gravy,» as one critic described his style, there was no denying of his considerable talent.[9] But, as another critic indignantly exclaimed, «It simply won't do to ignore a whole generation of progress towards the limits of abstraction, to deny surrealism, cubism,

Francisco de Goya: *Saturn*, 1721–23, Prado, Madrid.

Klee, Kandinsky, Picasso, Francis Bacon . . . It takes courage, however, to face up to one's own time, more courage than is needed to beat the baby drum of reactionism.»[10] Of course one could reject the art establishment's definition of «one's own time.» According to Nerdrum, one had to reject it, since it was no longer classical, but rather, modern art which constituted the tranquilizers for our times. And just as modern artists had ignored preceding centuries, he chose to ignore his own. It was not long before his extreme and extraordinary activities led to the label of «the Nerdrum phenomenon.»[11]

He could hardly have chosen a rockier road. There were no living traditions for this type of art, no educational opportunities. Other than consulting conservation experts to guide him in the choice of oils, grounds, and varnishes, he had to learn by trial and error. His choice of such a demanding and eccentric style was very precarious, both in terms of the demand for craftsmanship and in the scant professional fellowship this career would offer. In retrospect he described himself as being «scared stiff all through the sixties.»[12] And at the Academy there would soon be a falling out with his first professor, Åge Storstein, who failed to see why this reluctant student insisted on returning to Rembrandt, «with Picasso still alive.»[13] Nerdrum switched professors, but following a few turbulent years he was «chased out of the Academy like a mangy dog,» as he put it later. When, in the same interview, he was asked to explain his choice of artistic ideals, he replied: «I have always found Rembrandt's world more humane than Picasso's . . . The lifespan of a work of art is proportional to its human content.»[14]

Nerdrum's unconventional choice of ideals would scarcely be a strong selling point with his next professor, Joseph Beuys, at the academy of art in Düsseldorf. And yet, in 1965, when he followed the suggestion of his friend Arne Paus, a student of Beuys's, and submitted an application with ten drawings in the classical, figurative style, he was admitted. Nerdrum soon realized that his final attempt at learning something from within the new, academic form of modernism was a mistake. Here everything was permitted and nothing impossible – except painting like the old masters. His fellow students nicknamed him «Zorn,» from the notorious Swedish «flesh-painter,» and his three months in Düsseldorf left him feeling at least as

isolated as back home in Oslo. On a personal level he had, however, developed a very good rapport with his teacher. Beuys resembled Bjørneboe in his anarchistic attitude and his anthroposophist leanings, and Nerdrum liked him. Privately Beuys often showed concern for the young Norwegian, despite the fact that he constituted an artistic problem and was much too «narrow,» as he later reported to his American gallerist, Ronald Feldman.[15] Seventeen years would pass before their next meeting, and Beuys changed his mind.

Another one of the sixties celebrities Nerdrum met, Andy Warhol, never did change his opinion. He had none. In December 1968, after having been selected by an artists' organization, Nerdrum went to New York for his first one-man show abroad – at the SAS offices on Fifth Avenue. Concerned that they might encourage a fear of flying, the management prohibited him from showing three of his paintings. The day after the opening he cancelled the exhibition and removed his works. He was not in the highest of spirits when the Norwegian photographer Robert Meyer, who had accompanied Nerdrum in order to document his visit, brought him along for a visit to Warhol's Factory. When Nerdrum got around to telling Warhol that he painted in the style of the old masters, one of the assistants smirked. But Warhol brushed the insult aside with his laconic: «That's ok. Why not?»[16] Seeing Warhol's «postmodern» indifference only strengthened Nerdrum's anti-modernist position. And a few years later, when he painted his second version of *Amputation* (4), one of the three paintings censored in New York, there was an unmistakable resemblance to Warhol in the figure of man amputated by technology. Although Nerdrum has always denied that this was done intentionally, there is no doubt that Warhol – as the self-proclaimed «art machine» he was – had long been a central symbol of the role of art and artists in his time. Throughout the sixties Nerdrum seized every opportunity to launch verbal attacks on this role and on the ideals of his time, before he reached for his pen and formulated his agenda in a two-part essay in 1972. In the first part, entitled «'The New' in Art,» he asserted that «Our time is the age of fragmentation . . . The spirit of unification is gone.»[17] In part two he elaborated:

*Today the world resides in a spiritual darkness. Not only
Europe suffers doubt. The entire world gropes for spiritual re-
newal. What happened, what started the annihilation of
«beauty» – and what created the grotesque mask of empty and
affected vices in our culture?*
*I believe I have the diagnosis: It was the tremendous develop-
ment of rational science and finally its total conquest of the
human mind in our century . . . Our parents' generation consisted of devoted admirers and worshippers of rational science.
To them the future meant the technologically rational triumph
over nature. Few of them realized that the age of technology is
a substitute world, which replaced the world of «faith and nature.»*
*All genuine forms of art have suffered under the rational way
of thinking of this new age . . . Instead of suffering a decent
demise by maintaining a patient sincerity towards nature, art
has chosen such a pathetic course that the result can only be
sad. Art chooses to submit to the demands of a technological
age of reason; and as a consequence there is now more superficial art being produced than ever before . . . The artist has
fallen victim to rationalization, becoming a useless individual; he can at best achieve the social position of a decorator, a
mascot, or a nuisance.*
*People of today have never really seen themselves recreated,
and therefore lack a visual sense of self. Their depiction is always done indirectly or directly through the photograph . . .
But the image of their innermost selves apparently no longer
exists . . .*
*In the blinded state man finds himself in today I still believe
in the future potential of visual art – for the wondrous and
contradictory thoughts and movements of this world provide
opportunities for other worlds than the one of rational
foolishness.»*[18]

Nerdrum's refusal to accept the conditions of a rational and
fragmented age not only explains his need to reject modernism, but above all it points to his choice of Rembrandt as
his ideal. To Nerdrum this painter came to personify the
unified world, predating «rational foolishness,» a world in
which the painted darkness was spiritual and not a spiritual
darkness. Ever since the time of Plato and up until the se-
venteenth century Goodness, Truth, and Beauty had been
regarded as absolute values, an indivisible whole. During
Rembrandt's lifetime this view of the world began to crum-

ble under the pressure of rationalist philosophers such as
Bacon and Descartes; and when Newton published his
*Principia* eighteen years after the death of Rembrandt in
1669, the new scientific view of the world was ready to take
over. At least as important was the new concept of nature.
The Descartian philosophy of reason would lead to an ever
greater subordination of nature in favor of the reasoning
subject. Nature, and consequently the body, would from
now on be seen as the antithesis of reason. Nature still constituted a force, however, and it was the task of science to
harness it, in the same way that rational thought was to
tame human nature. Man was to control the environment
by means of technology and his body by means of reason.

It was the last remainder of the old world view
Nerdrum had rediscovered in the tenebrism of Rembrandt.
He represented the live human being against cold technology, emotion and imagination against one-dimensional
reason, and nature against a rational culture. And more
than that. Rembrandt had consciously rejected the fashio-
nable trends of his time and had gone his own way. The
painting of *Claudius Civilis*, which had so fascinated
Nerdrum in Stockholm, was indeed the very last public
commission Rembrandt got; and in 1662, after only a year
on the wall in the Amsterdam city hall, it was removed and
replaced by a more conventional history painting by one of
his former pupils. Rembrandt's Descartes-influenced critics
disapproved of his insistence that his artistic freedom be
left unchecked by any overriding idea. They could not
accept his painting human nature as he perceived it instead
of the way rational art trends dictated it to be. To them he
was «art's greatest heretic.»[19] But Nerdrum saw him as a
role model, especially in his tenacity in living up to his
artistic commitments. Despite humiliation and poverty he
did not yield. Rembrandt was the outsider and the exception in a world of fawning conformists, and a painter
Nerdrum could identify with when he in turn had been
branded as a heretic and had broken with the stylistic con-
ventions of his own time.

Although his historical retreat had certain nostalgic un-
dertones, Nerdrum's project was well considered. In his criticism of reason he entered an enduring intellectual and artistic tradition with roots as far back as the Romantics.
One of the first to give voice to this view was the painter
and poet William Blake, who in the early 1800s claimed

4. *Amputation,* 1968 – 1974. 76 ¾ x 101 ½ in.

that man had been robbed of his vision of unity, since:

*The Reasoning Spectre*
*Stands between the Vegetative Man*
*& His Immortal Imagination.*[20]

Fifty years later the poet Charles Baudelaire followed his example of critique of reason and an advocacy of unity, in which he sought to combine the tangible outer world with the spiritual inner world, by an approach that pre-dated Descartes. Baudelaire's aesthetics provided the basis for the modern tradition the Futurists and the Dadaists pushed to its ultimate limit before the end of World War I, when they engaged in their irrational art sabotage as a means to restore mental and cultural balance. As one of them put it: «The myth that everything in the world can be rationally explained had been gaining ground since the time of Descartes. An inversion was necessary to restore the balance.»[21] According to Nerdrum, however, the desperate strategy of this sabotage was merely an inevitable conse-

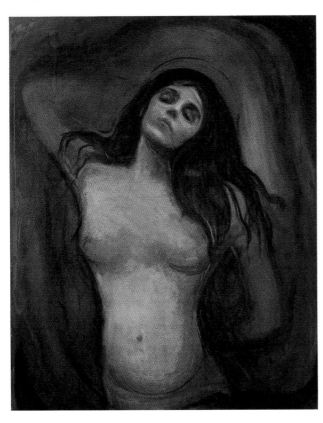

quence of «the demands of the age of reason» and incapable of providing us with any visual alternative. Man and nature were as distant in this kind of art as they were in Malevich's empty squares and Mondrian's grids. A major focus of the modern avant-garde was to invalidate classical art by denying the spectator any physical recognition in his encounters with their new and shocking art objects, just as the Futurists in their food manifesto would conclude the work with their many fanciful recipes by denying the dinner guests the chance to eat the food. The only possible way out, as far as Nerdrum could see, was an inversion of everything modernism stood for.

Nerdrum's ambition was instead to ethically restore man through an aesthetic re-creation – to offer him a visual impression of himself that was not conveyed through photography or other mechanical means of reproduction. This is why he reached back to a representational art, created by direct visual investigation and invariably using models. Rembrandt and the classical tradition became a means rather than an end: «The old masters are my guides, nature is my God.»[22] This nature was, however, quite specific: «I am no worshipper of nature in the sense of our National Romantics. What I seek to bring out is the higher being in nature . . . A painting ought to be a window onto a world – into a world – where the truest and simplest ideas reside . . . To me it is imperative to use the simplest of means in order to speak of the best in man and of his sufferings, longings, and hopes. Everything I do should be judged by the human in man.»[23]

Using this as a background for placing the early Nerdrum in the anti-rational and unity-seeking tradition, he would be found where Blake's transcendental romanticism of longing meets Baudelaire's more subterranean nostalgia of suffering. His second version of *Hermaphrodite* (5), in which he has painted himself in the posture of Munch's *Madonna* but with the anatomy of Michelangelo's *Dying Slave*, shows some of the same origins (fig.). Both Blake and Baudelaire were influenced by the occult mystic Emanuel Swedenborg, who believed to have found – within an alchemist outlook – the lost unity of opposites, in which man and nature, mind and matter, were parts of the same organic whole. One of the manifestations of this idea of unity was the bisexual androgyne, or hermaphrodite, whom Nerdrum now used to present the feminine «anima»

Edvard Munch: *Madonna,* 1894–1895. Nasjonalgalleriet, Oslo.
Michelangelo: *Dying Slave,* Louvre, Paris.

**5.** *Hermaphrodite,* 1965 – 1981. 57 ½ x 39 ½ in.

ways be subject to his sex and body, having to cope with this – being dependent on an earthbound body. To this I have always remained faithful.»[24]

In Nerdrum's opinion there was no spiritual dimension beyond that inhabiting matter. He represented this by painting tangibly and physically present bodies, unmistakably strutting of flesh and blood. Without sensually plausible and convincingly portrayed human bodies consisting of mass, weight, and a living, textured skin, there could be no credible mind where the shifting «sufferings, longings, and hopes» of life could unfold; and there would be nothing for us, looking at the paintings, to recognize as genuinely human. This is also why it was mostly his contemporaries he found beautiful – living their lives and expressing their feelings – so long as they did not assume «the perennial social posture thought by pretty models to constitute the essence of their personality.»[25] Nerdrum wanted to show man's «innermost self» – to provide us with a «mirror of the soul.»

The mirrored soul he would most often show was, as in Rembrandt's case, his own. Against a backdrop of unabashed self-worship – as in the declaration: «I am the hero of my own life»[26] – most of his many self-portraits have gotten a somewhat elevated and arrogant look, the head tilted slightly back and being seen from a somewhat lower angle. This is a feature found not only in self-portraits by Botticelli and the young Munch, but in great measure borrowed from Delacroix's and Courbet's romantic depictions of the spiritual depths of the artistic genius. In Nerdrum's *Self-Portrait with Hat* (6) he also displays his formal affinity with this role of the artist by painting himself in a contemporary version of the outfit worn by Courbet in his *Self-Portrait with Black Dog* (fig.). And confirmation that some of this romantic ideal of the artist had long been a substantial part of his self-image may be found in a photograph taken in 1968 by Robert Meyer in Nerdrum's studio – in which he is seated in front of a reproduction of Watts's *Hope* (fig.). The painter's staff and cape is there and even the dog as a companion for the searching loner.

In addition to these heartfelt mirrors of the soul, Nerdrum in the sixties painted a number of mythical and visionary paraphrases, often carrying titles borrowed from Greek and Roman mythology. In 1967 he spoke of the present he wanted to reflect: «I view it from a diagnostic angle

in his psyche, and thus himself as a «whole» human being. Unlike his predecessors, however, he was not interested in turning his desire for unity into pure metaphysics. In referring to «the higher being in nature,» he did not mean the divine or a beyond, but our concrete and earthbound mind. «The problem,» he maintained, «is that man will al-

Gustave Courbet: *Self-Portrait with Black Dog*, 1840 – 44. Museé du Petit Palais, Paris
Robert Meyer: *Portrait of Odd Nerdrum,* 1968. Oslo

6. *Self-Portrait with Hat,* 1979. 31 ½ x 30 ¾ in.

. . . I try to depict the world in which we live and the one yet to come.»[27] Our world he diagnosed in *Amputation, Isolation*, and *Madonna Losing Her Child.* The one to come would be no improvement, and his response to the suggestion that we take our protein pills, put our helmets on, and set off, seemed clear. For here man floated about, naked and alone, in the outer space recently conquered by rational science or was about to crash, winglessly, to the ground, as in another of Nerdrum's foreboding soarers, *Icharos.* The attitude he showed in these allegories, clearly anti-utopian and critical of our civilization, had apparently been kindled by his dream of recovering something more basic and enduring. In the sixties it had, however, also been influenced by a more pessimistic source: Oswald Spengler's theory of the rise, prime, and fall of civilizations, in *The Decline of the West*, which appeared in 1918. The book had made a strong impression on Nerdrum, who, against a backdrop of gloomy sunsets or dark rooms, painted isolated, melancholy figures standing within a symbolic realm of the mind, between one world vanishing and another about to appear. About 1981, as the dream of escaping a bleak future gradually took another direction in his work,

he would return to this ambiguous twilight world with greater force. But for the time being, and through most of the seventies, he would concentrate on a more down-to-earth depiction of his times, as well as on the technical means of expression offered him by classical art.

In referring to the old masters as his guides, Rembrandt served as Nerdrum's principal guide. Yet, in time, his frame of reference came to include a number of artists from Masaccio of the early Renaissance to Käthe Kollwitz, a twentieth century exception. To Nerdrum classical tradition was not limited to a narrowly defined historical style, including instead the entire heritage of antiquity, which had been reborn in the Renaissance and had been brought to an end with Cezanne at the end of the nineteenth century. Within this range anything was possible, though not equally desirable. The canonical and idealized version found in Neoclassicism was of no interest to him. Instead he sought more profound, at times also more dramatic, depths of the human soul, as well as in nature. These he found in artists such as Leonardo, Michelangelo, and the late Titian, in Goya and Chardin, as well as in «heavy» Romantics, such as Gericault and Millet, in other words, all those who reminded him, of Rembrandt. However, Nerdrum also included elements from Norwegian romanticism and the symbolism of Lars Hertervig and the early Munch, or, as evident in some of his landscapes, elements from German romanticism and Nordic naturalism.

On a trip to Rome in 1968 Nerdrum had discovered the baroque realist Caravaggio, the first of the old masters to paint nature «the way it was.» Besides Rembrandt, who was himself influenced by Caravaggio, no one had the same power to influence Nerdrum in his early career as this radical chiaroscuro painter. It had all started in 1964 with Nerdrum's first exhibition, when his friend, the sculptor Per Ung, drew the attention of his older classical colleague Joseph Grimeland to Nerdrum's paintings. Grimeland was both impressed and heartened at the sight; and when they met, a couple of years later, a long-lasting friendship developed. Grimeland became both a new father figure and a mentor to Nerdrum, and he was the one to introduce Nerdrum to Caravaggio in Rome: «In San Luigi dei Francesi it was as though lightening had struck me. It was a confrontation with my own longing . . . I felt reborn in his dramatic, naked view of man.»[28]

Caravaggio: *Flagellation of Christ,* Pinoteca di Capodimonte, Napoli

7. *The Murder of Andreas Baader,* 1977 – 78. 130 x 106 ¼ in.

Following an initial, almost socialist-realist period, Caravaggio's influence increased throughout the seventies. Nerdrum, whose painting had all along shown concern for outsiders and victimized individuals, often allowed his engagement to shine through in his treatment of everything from «free love» to mental illness and the abuse of power. The more provocative and politically incorrect his theme, the better. An example of this is *The Murder of Andreas Baader* (7), which he significantly painted while writing *Havfuglen* [*The Seabird*], and which had a clear allusion to his own role as victim in the relationship with his stepfather. Baader was a German leftist terrorist believed by Nerdrum to have been incapable of committing suicide in jail. As a declared anarchist, Nerdrum felt obliged to defend him as a «victim» of the establishment. His compositional solution was based on the cross of St. Andrew, extended into an almost complete swastika by means of body postures and the direction of the guard's gaze. Despite the fact that the figure of Baader came to resemble Michelangelo's Florence *Pieta* and Dutch baroque depositions from the cross more than it did any of Caravaggio's figures, the influence of Caravaggio is still visible in the immediate presence of the figures and in the dramatic cuts created by the sharp contrast between light and shadow in the picture. But this theatrical, almost operatic pathos resulting from Nerdrum's strong empathy with the violent painter gradually gave way to the more lasting interest he had in the pulsating and «meaty» depiction of flesh, where the bodies appeared as substances hit by the light from another world. This technique – the sfumato of the blurred contour lines, the insistent sensuality in the rendering of flesh, as well as such rounded body forms as those found in the painting *Back* (8) – is still one of the most characteristic features in Nerdrum's paintings, and one which clearly distinguished him from other painters working in the classical figurative tradition around the world.

Only weeks remained of the seventies when Nerdrum began the work that would be the final history painting dramatizing a contemporary event – *Refugees at Sea* (9). When the painting was finished, in the summer of 1980, after six months of intensive studies of numerous models, it was one of the most ambitious and complicated classical figure compositions ever done in Norwegian art, and also the largest painting made by Nerdrum. The subject is a group of twenty-seven Vietnamese refugees, who, after much longing and suffering, set out onto the sea of hope in a small, over-crowded junk. In the twilight is the ominous calm before the storm. Emotions and attitudes are reflected on the faces and in the bodies, much as in Jacob Jordaens's painting *The Ferryboat to Antwerp* (fig.), which Nerdrum had seen on his youthful excursions to Copenhagen. In the dusk to the right he has placed the picture's main character, with whom he himself could identify – the helmsman with his right arm amputated, misfortune incarnate.

This grand painting became the highpoint of the realistic style that dominated Nerdrum's work in the seventies, including everything from the baroque drama of the Baader painting to the intimate, tender, and peaceful portraits of members of his family. He had gone as far as he could go in painting emotions in the sense of «mirrors of the soul,» no matter how sincere and how deeply held. A limit had been reached, and a long period was drawing to an end. A limit had also been reached in his status on the Norwegian art scene, where he remained a fairly isolated figure, even though he had been joined by a few other figurative painters and a number of young pupils. To those locked into a modernist regimen Nerdrum represented a clear provocation. His work was generally regarded as kitsch, hopelessly sentimental and reactionary kitsch. His ethical perspectives were taboo, and his old-fashioned style belonged solely in dusty museums. The problem was that his skills as a painter were undeniable – that he had gone from being what many saw as a fleeting phenomenon to being the leading representative of an alternative style. Granted, not many artists would take the trouble of learning it, but it could no longer be ignored. Nerdrum's feeling of artistic confinement in Norway soon led him to go abroad, and since 1984 he has exhibited mostly in the U.S. He still preferred to live and work in Oslo, however; and as long as this was possible, he saw no reason to pull up his roots and leave. In time the isolation became voluntary, and his private little war with all forms of modernity took a new direction, as he began exploring new areas of human existence in his paintings.

The large refugee painting convinced Nerdrum that he mastered the techniques needed to solve the greatest compositional challenges, and that he was now relatively skilled

8. *Back*, 1979. 86 ½ x 63 in.

in the craft he had decided to learn when he stood before Rembrandt's painting in Stockholm. Soon he would also come to regard this piece of work as the final test of his eighteen-year long apprenticeship. This was an important acknowledgement for his future career, enabling him to re-lax his very stringent demands for a correct stylistic rheto-ric and instead turn to other issues than the critique of rea-son inherent in his use of the style of the old masters. Thus Nerdrum ended his apprenticeship in the same way that his own life began – with people in flight. When he was to return to this theme again, man was no longer fleeing from one particular nation, but leaving an entire civilization.

The development leading up to this change in Nerdrum's outlook may be traced in three twilight scenes painted between 1979 and 1981. The final picture shows a drastic transformation of his views of man and nature. The starting point in this process may be seen in *Self-Portrait in the Evening Sun* (10). Dressed in a leather jacket and wear-ing a tattered headband, he has placed himself in the Nordic twilight, right in between the imperfect world of time and the perfect harmony of eternity. His expression still echoed verbal droppings from Baudelaire and was one of «pure yearning, graceful melancholy, and noble hope-lessness.»[29] In other words, Nerdrum found himself on the same spot where he had been since the sixties: in the pre-sent, harboring a dream of unity. His efforts to heal man using a classical spirituality had failed. After completing *Refugees at Sea*, in 1980, he realized that the problem lay in his view of man: «I shall never again make such a picture, because all the individuals on that raft cannot guarantee the qualities I gave them. I had made heroes of them all, beautiful saints wanting to do good. I was convinced that man was good. Since then I have come to see things diffe-rently. I do not believe that man is good, but that he can become good . . . I cannot continue to give villains my blessing by the way I paint them. The idea was naive.»[30]

Nerdrum was obviously disillusioned. Not on behalf of his old master's style, but rather on behalf of the rational contemporary man, living his life between good and evil on his way to a future that looked less enticing with each passing day. Something was wrong. It soon became clear that the problem could be traced to our consciousness. Throughout the critical tradition Nerdrum had become a part of, it had long been customary to blame the Descar-tian belief in reason and the rationalism of the Enlighten-ment for our longing for unity. But in the view Nerdrum was now approaching, rational philosophers could not be held responsible for man's clinging to such hopes. Man had yearned for this long before them. The problem seemed not to lie in the belief in reason itself, but in man's gift of an insatiable spiritual urge, in a perennial search for some-thing more complete and perfect than he could find within himself. Several thinkers had pointed to the futility of a re-turn to unity, but it was not until Jean-Paul Sartre, sitting in the occupied Paris in 1943, finishing his major existen-tialist work, *Being and Nothingness*, that the problem was fully addressed.

Sartre believed that the fully conscious individual had never been «whole» or «total,» and never would be. In his view our consciousness is split between reason and rationa-lity on the one hand, and another mental category causing us to feel the abyss of loss and to long for unity on the other. These two aspects depended on one another and were indivisible. Eliminating the «reasoning spectre» was impossible, and merging the two categories into a qualita-tively higher unity, as many had hoped for, he called «the impossible synthesis.»[31] This dimension of unity we longed for was, according to Sartre, a product of our own con-sciousness, and a sign of a permanent absence within our selves that could never be filled. We were thrown into a fu-tile search for a totality never to be achieved, unless we lost that which constituted us as seeking beings: our very con-sciousness. «But,» stated Sartre, «consciousness does not surpass itself toward its annihilation: it does not want to lose itself . . .»[32] And this was at the crux of Nerdrum's new-found position. For what seemed to trouble him in man was the hopelessly divided consciousness in which we find ourselves trapped, and which even the most advanced New Age techniques cannot make us relinquish. This was the same consciousness that for thousands of years had in-

Jacob Jordaen: *The Ferry*, ca. 1623. Statens Museum for Kunst, København.

**9.** *Refugees at Sea,* 1979 – 1980. 132 ¾ x 200 ¾ in.

cessantly propelled man, farther and farther away from «the human in man,» and ever more removed from the very nature that had been our origin. It may have spawned all that he valued as great and beautiful in the arts, but ultimately it had also killed it.

If Descartes and the Enlightenment could not be held responsible for our problematic consciousness, when and where did it appear? When was the «fall from grace?» The German philosophers Horkheimer and Adorno believed the answer could be found as far back as in the literary foundation of Western civilization – *The Odyssey*. According to their joint *Dialectic of Enlightenment* – written in exile from Hitler's Germany and published in New York in the year of Nerdrum's birth – «disaster triumphant» illuminated our fully enlightened and rationally governed world. They had located the start of this development in the cradle of our civilization – Greece in the eighth century B.C. and in the heroic character of Ulysses. He was the first human being in written history – that is: as long as we have used concepts formed by the aid of a phonetic alphabet – who by the use of language, reason, and a newly developed self-awareness had learnt to deceive the gods and nature in order to live a little longer than the time allotted him by Fate. It is only at this point in history that man develops a consciousness that, like our own, is divided between a self-preserving reason, governed by words and concepts, and a void left by the gods and nature, holding nothing but a longing for an eternally lost, primordial unity. Ulysses himself tells of how he saw his crew revert to a pre-rational, natural state of harmony in the company of the Lotus-Eaters, but that he then went ashore and forcibly brought his weeping mates back to the ship, where he chained them. Like all civilized men he feared a loss of his own consciousness, but he left the alluring land «grieving still at heart.»[33] Ulysses was the start of everything that Nerdrum would now turn upside-down in his imagery. Ever since the sixties he had, through his depiction of the emotions caused by our split consciousness, tried to recreate a true image of man. This was only half the truth, though. Now he wanted to attempt a recreation of the underlying, the original, and «eternal» truth about man – the timeless.

Some time later, when Nerdrum was asked to comment on his *Self-Portrait in the Evening Sun*, he explained: «I re-

member when I was a child and saw the sun setting on the long beaches – there was twilight. The motorboats stopped and the birds fell silent. That is when I saw the reflection of timelessness in nature, something I later rediscovered in Renaissance and baroque art. The hour of timelessness – the hour of twilight – is the hour I have been preoccupied with.»[34] In this picture he had not, however, painted the «reflection of timelessness in nature» that he had once perceived. Instead he had painted the reflection of timelessness as it became an urge in his own consciousness, while standing there looking at us in the dusky twilight. And this was different. Nature's own timelessness, along with the truly timeless in man, was not the same as the self-centered consciousness of our civilization. But it was this insight he expressed in a rather drastic way in 1981, when he painted his monumental defecation scene *Twilight* (11). In it he portrays a woman performing a basic bodily function, as natural, organic, and timeless as the primal forest she squats in. Although she belongs to our own time, there is no mistaking what is timeless in man. The head is turned away and hidden. The last rays of evening sun penetrate the dense forest, illuminating a body that is simply obeying its own nature, not the bidding of the mind. Nerdrum had seen a similar incident in a loft once and now repeated it on canvas, as «a tribute to the natural, the true human being, whom we all fear.»[35]

With *Twilight* Nerdrum used a totally new approach to the problematic relationship between man, the function of his consciousness, and nature. He acknowledged our divided mind and gave up his striving for «the impossible synthesis» of the unity-seeking tradition. He seemed to accept the mind as in fact different from nature, as Descartes had so emphatically argued, but he reversed his value emphasis by putting nature and the natural first. The tangible nature that had represented his «god» in the sixties had no autonomous existence outside its manifestation in the mind, just as he in earlier paintings had looked upon human nature as an emotionally laden mind tied to the body. But when he declares, at the start of the eighties, that: «Nature is the only thing I trust,»[36] his concept of nature has acquired a more general meaning. In his artistic universe he now increasingly begins to see nature as an eternal process in matter itself, whereby it is not only a separate entity, but it is also given a higher inherent value than the type of con-

10. *Self-Portrait in the Evening Sun,* 1977–79. 33 ¼ x 27 ¼ in.

sciousness that can recognize or reject it according to pre-ference. To the Romantics nature was an object of wor-ship. To Nerdrum it became instead a guide, which in its very functional necessity would always have the last word against our civilizing consciousness. As he put it: «In the long run nature always wins.»[37] From now on it is nature as such that represents the ultimate goodness and truth to him, and, not least, the only truly beautiful, since *Twilight*, as he pointed out, was also painted for the pur-pose of «expanding people's concept of beauty.»[38]

Not everyone appreciated this expansion of the con-cept of beauty. Nerdrum was seen to not only turn his back on the world, but to frankly signal that he would willingly defecate on his critics and the Norwegian art scene. But when Beuys saw the painting, he smelt more than the old-fashioned paint. Beuys had been preoccupied with nature throughout his career and had often used ani-mals and various protective or healing natural products in his survival-mythological objects. But, according to his biographers, this was for the purpose of expressing the «original unity of reason and intuition,»[39] which Nerdrum was now beginning to doubt. In September 1982 Beuys was in Oslo for an exhibition, and after having accompa-nied Nerdrum around the city to have a look at his vari-ous pictures from the seventies, he finally came to the stu-dio, where *Twilight* was being stored. Seeing this tribute to nature, he declared this to be the most radical painting he had ever seen. As a result Beuys changed his opinion of Nerdrum's work, now convinced that «something impor-tant would come out of it.»[40] To Nerdrum, however, the

extreme human naturalism of *Twilight* only marked the start of his new course. He had not yet reached the end of his radical line.

Nerdrum had allowed his choice of subject matter to be guided solely by nature's own organic processes. In terms of form it seemed that the rhetoric used by the old masters in their rendering of nature still represented more of its reflection of timelessness than Nerdrum had so far allowed nature's own forms to do. However, one composi-tional element in *Twilight* is totally new in his figure pain-ting – and soon to be integrated in his art – an element that becomes clear when studying his method of making the female figure appear monumental. Except for a few minor natural deviations she is completely symmetrically drawn on the picture's vertical mid-axis and is placed alto-gether below the horizontal one. The lines of her body create a number of triangles, focusing our attention and visually balancing the figure. This was a method of com-position frequently used by Caspar David Friedrich in his romantic landscapes, though with the intention of letting his tiny centralized figures express man's insignificance in relation to «God's sublime nature.» Nerdrum applies this symmetrical principle for the opposite purpose. His soli-tary, brightly lit figure is instead enthroned in the center of the foreground, close and tangible. What he sought to elevate was the true and natural human being – to make the profane sacred. Fifteen years were to pass before Nerdrum would once again sacralize such a profane scene, but the direction of the change in his art was now set.

11. *Twilight*, 1981. 77 ½ x 102 ½ in.

# THE MENTAL REFUGE

THE INITIAL SIGNS OF A CHANGE IN ODD NER-drum's work appeared in 1982, as he started painting bricks, dentures, and babies (12–14). In these works he completely isolates his objects. The surrounding space lies in mute darkness, without any local definitions. The darkness gives the space a timeless quality, which is transmitted to the simple, highlighted object. Nerdrum read a great deal of Kant in this period, but these are hardly pure objects of thought – the thing-in-itself. On the contrary, he chose a brick in order to bring out the specific character of that particular brick, making it tangibly present for us. He wanted to render its individuality in a setting that left it undisturbed by any extraneous elements, a place beyond time and space, in which it could rest in itself and express nothing but its own substance. To Nerdrum it was precisely this simple and naked truth inherent in the object itself that constituted its beauty: «Beauty is a moment of cognition. It needs to have no beauty of its own . . . : When I was a child and my great-grandmother's sister died, I opened a drawer in her room and saw a set of dentures. It frightened me. Two years ago I got hold of some dentures and began to paint them. I tried to revive that memory and realized how redeemingly beautiful those dentures were.»[1]

Time and again Nerdrum now found himself returning to the atmosphere and experience of his childhood. The images rising to the surface from his recollections slowly began to break loose from the patterns of the old masters by which his forms had earlier been bound. He saw himself as having been «for many years in the role of an apprentice. Always studying. It has been an almost morbid identification with the greatest paintings ever made. I feel that I am close to working my way out of it now.»[2] One of the clearest signs that something was about to happen can be seen in *The Baby*, first painted in 1982, when the second of his three daughters was born, and then repeated with every new child born until 1995.[3]

Ever since childhood darkness had held a special fascination for Nerdrum. He loved having Bjørneboe as his teacher, because «he appreciated the power of darkness,

turned out the light and told us ghost stories in order to draw us into the great darkness.»[4] In the preceding paintings of objects he had associated this darkness with a timeless space; but starting with his first version of *The Baby*, it also took on a new meaning in his visual vocabulary: «To me darkness means security,» he says, enclosing the sleeping child in darkness as if it were a substance of its own, as protective of the child's physical being as the old-fashioned swaddle he has put around it, which is the main symbol of security in the painting. This cocoon-like wrapping seems to protect the child in the same manner as organic life forms are protected in nature – the butterfly-to-be in its chrysalis and the flower-to-be in the bud. Such shapes directly inspired by nature cannot be found in his earlier pictures.

Although bundled figures and swaddled babies were hardly new motifs in the history of art, Nerdrum's symbolic use of these forms took a unique direction. The mummy-like, or naturally rounded, blunted shapes, would come to express not only security but also the object's own substantial value. The darkness surrounding the child was simply a metaphor for this material substance, as it appeared in the brick paintings. A substantial form, on the other hand, was something that freed the painted substance from its surroundings and made it independent of other substances. Placing the object on its own was not sufficient to give it an aura of timelessness. It also had to have a certain rounded and enclosed shape, which made it rest securely in itself within its natural boundaries, expressing nothing but its own substance. This was the type of substantial shape he had given *The Baby*, lying there enclosed as a mother would protect her child and the way nature protects its budding life: «Everything is to be enshrined in itself,» he explained. «Then man is at his greatest and most beautiful.»[5] And just as it had been in *Twilight*, it was clear that in Nerdrum's new universe man did not receive his ultimate value from his ability to express our culturally conditioned form of consciousness, but, rather, from his ability to act according to his innate and more timeless nature. The new dimension lay in

12. *White Brick,* 1984. 16 ½ x 21 ¾ in.

**13.** *Dentures,* 1983. 12 ¼ x 15 ½ in.

Nerdrum's having found a shape he could give to his true and natural human being: «Not until recently have I understood where I am heading in this world. I have begun to grasp the forms of nature. My task is to clarify life in a way that adds to what has been created before. Nature is no longer man's adversary – it is man's salvation.»[6]

In *Portrait of a Child* (15), painted in 1982 and clearly influenced by Rembrandt, Nerdrum has obviously made use of the blunted and rounded shapes in order to unify and simplify the appearance of the figure. The beautiful, sexless being stands naked, save for the cloak wrapped around and gathered in the hands. A headband holds the curly hair in a circle, which accentuates the rounded shape of the head. There is, however, a new expression on the face – not seen in earlier portraits by Nerdrum. A gentle, clarified, and open expression with the vague hint of a smile. Nerdrum has released the child from the present. One can sense a timeless look in the eyes, devoid of desire.

Nerdrum continued to develop his characters in this direction. The head of *Sigmund in Red Coat* (16) is now all wrapped in leather bands, his hands hidden beneath the cloth. Nerdrum shows a similarly protective use of form in *Portrait of a Girl* (17), a motif entitled *Anine* in the first version, from 1985. The rounded shape of her head is repeated in the stumped hand and in the relatively modern canteen, whose screw cap is attached by a strap, a form echoed in the small protruding end of the headband. The background is curved at the bottom in a way that leaves doubt as to whether she is painted against a piece of cloth or a piece of ground. Despite all the accessories and a convincing craftsmanship invested in fabric and flesh, time does not seem to have let go of these figures. It has, however, released *Isola* (18), which, perhaps more than any of the other characters he conceived around 1984, testifies to his new attitude: «Our time is worthless as a basis for visual representation.»[7]

The name «Isola» may connote either «isolation» or «island,» as the Italian word means. An oft-cited phrase claims that no man is an island. In Nerdrum's version, however, this is precisely what this individual is. Her presence in the large, dark space is as tangible and timeless as that of the brick, and as secure and substantial as that of the baby. A pure and undisturbed being that makes the figure autonomous and free. The soft, rounded shapes also

seem more natural in relation to this stoic individual, standing there, enclosing herself. But somehow the open expression on her face seems encapsulated, as well. Nerdrum has isolated her in her own, distant world, closed to us. In her clear, wet eyes we cannot detect any emotion or other expression with which we can identify. She does not direct her attention to us, and neither attempts to communicate nor to hide anything. No secrets, no desire. No longing, no suffering. He has painted her as if she were an island of the mind, far removed from our own mentality, with no visible signs of the inner dialogue taking place in a conscious human being.

In terms of visual forms Nerdrum had now occupied a realm far removed from the old masters. There are details in the appearance of these figures that may recall medieval paintings; but one has to go even farther back to find parallels to the consistent, stylized look Nerdrum has now created by his use of substantial shapes. Looking at the stiff, clearly «anti-classical» frontality of *Isola* – her broad forehead and the sharply drawn, wide-open eyes – and comparing this with an archaic Greek sculpture, one will find identical features. Ulysses' descendants were not, however, the originators of this style. It was a legacy from Egypt, and it was Nerdrum's early interest in Egyptian art that had now been rekindled. The Egyptians frequently made their figures with the left foot forward. Limbs were kept close to the body, and the hands were firmly clenched – in some cases also underneath the cloth. On a small stone sculpture made around 2400 B.C., a so-called reserve-head, which accompanied the dead into the grave, we also recognize a type of headdress very similar to *Isola*'s white hood.[8]

This seemed to remove any doubt as to where Nerdrum was taking his characters. His search for what he called «the natural, the true human being» had led him, visually and mentally, to an era considerably predating Ulysses' «fall from grace.» *Isola* was a being intended to express a mind different from our own. Nerdrum may have seen her as the visualization of an ideal – an ideal that had not yet betrayed its own nature, as Ulysses had and as modern man continued to do in the name of progress. She was different, standing there as a monument to her own true nature. *Isola* represented the very archetype of existential man, whom Nerdrum had now reconstructed in

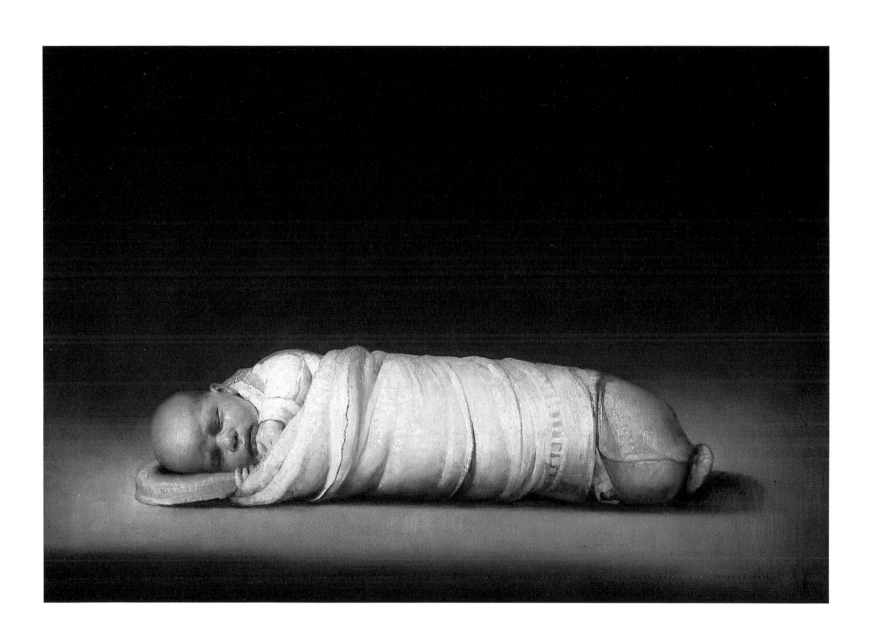

14. *The Baby,* 1982 – 1995. 22 ¾ x 33 ½ in.

**15.** *Portrait of a Child,* 1982. 63 x 44 in.

**16.** *Sigmund in Red Coat,* 1983 – 1995. 57 ½ x 45 ¾ in.

17. *Portrait of a Girl,* 1985 – 1995. 53 x 47 ½ in.

18. *Isola,* 1984 – 1995. 105 ½ x 68 in.

**19.** *Summer Day,* 1982. 59 x 88 ½ in.

the form of an archaic type of being.

It was only to be expected that the transformation now taking place in Nerdrum's art would also affect his landscapes. But this would take time. Landscape painting had always been of secondary importance in his work, and it was only in the summertime, while he was staying at his country house, that he painted in the open. In the early eighties he generally painted bright, open seashores in a romantic-naturalistic style. Preferably bathers, as in *Summer Day* (19), which gave free reign to his interest in naked bodies and intricate composition. Not until 1984 would there be a change in this area; but once the transformation began, it developed rapidly.

*Early Morning* (21), which was to be his last bathing scene, shows the inadequacy of this setting for what he wanted to convey through his figures. The landscape is grand and tranquil, but has an atmosphere of our own time, primarily due to the jet's vapor trail running across the clear sky. This painting is, however, of compositional interest – apart from the stiffly painted log, which might have been handled differently. All lines, except for the shoreline, whose curved diagonal mirrors the contrail, are vertical or horizontal. The figures are clustered in a shape that makes a right-angled U in the center of the picture. Within this grouping Nerdrum has placed them in a simple, mathematical relationship to one another in a ratio of one to one or one to two. The standing figures are based on a principle of singularity and are painted «one-legged» in a straight profile. Between these two he has placed a couple of seated, almost identical women, whose legs and shadows make up the horizontal base of the U-shape and whose torsos form the vertical axes in the middle. However, in order

to achieve linear harmony between the figures within the U-shape, Nerdrum has once again deliberately left out the shadow cast on the water by the bathing woman. In order to gain a numerical ratio between the seated twin figures – a double image already familiar from the backs in *Refugees at Sea* – he has cut the left leg off the nearest woman, so that the remaining leg relates to the other woman's two legs, like each of the standing figures to the two seated ones. A fairly intricate arrangement.

Then darkness descended on Nerdrum's seashores, and the landscapes began to change. In *The Evening Star* (22) he has added elements from both Caspar David Friedrich and Edvard Munch, but perhaps even more from the painting *Borgøya* by Lars Hertervig – a Norwegian Romantic Nerdrum was preoccupied with at the time (fig.). Before a slightly curved horizon a mother holding her child stands watching her counterpart on the firmament – a single star. One of the intentions behind this scene was to show man's individual and always equally solitary existence as a «lighthouse in the darkness.»[9] But unlike *Isola*, which in large measure possessed this quality, *The Evening Star* lost some of its intent. Its elements were all too naturalistic and site-specific to create the timeless and autonomous presence intended. The problem recurred in *Man in Abandoned Landscape* (23), a subject matter first painted in 1968, together with his other mythical visions of the future.[10] The naked, hunched figure is here entering a starry stone-age landscape that is well-furnished with «explanatory» details such as the caves in the rock and the pieces of old wood on the ground. Despite the fact that Nerdrum has not yet managed to solve the problem of his landscapes, he is clearly moving in the same direction as with *Isola*. For this is, according to a comment he made at the time, «modern man having returned to a primeval society in his flight from civilization. He no longer has any roots in our time. He is back in a prehistoric existence.»[11]

So Nerdrum is once again painting people in flight, but for completely different reasons than in 1980. The confused and vulnerable look of this figure indicates that the flight from the present has not been easy. Nerdrum himself explains that he created this new world to show modern man «after he has rebelled and fled our civilization in order to create a world of his own.»[12] And his reason for driving him «out onto the plains . . . to the starting point,» as he

Lars Hertervig: *Borgøya,* 1867. Nasjonalgalleriet, Oslo.

20. *Man with Headband*, 1982. 59 x 88 ½ in.

**21.** *Early Morning,* 1984. 61 x 94 ½ in.

23. *Man in Abandoned Landscape,* 1968 – 1984. 48 x 65 in.

**22.** *The Evening Star,* 1984. 35 ½ x 43 ¼ in.

not just a matter of shedding one's fashions, dropping out, and running off. Before man could return to this socially and psychologically natural state it apparently demanded a heavy toll. The price consisted of a submission to a painful ritual he called the *Iron Law* (24), or, as he characterized this scene: «I have certain apocalyptic impressions from childhood that I try to recall and put into my pictures.»[14] It is not impossible to regard this image as a metaphor for his wish to escape the pain inflicted upon him by his own life and still being inflicted simply through living in a civilization such as our own. Another suggestion of what this law entails may be found in Masaccio's fresco *Expulsion from Paradise*, which clearly must have been one of the sources for this painting (fig.). The distressed appearance of Adam's naked figure is related not only to the figures in *Iron Law*, but also to the man in the «abandoned landscape.» And looking at the «natural shapes» formed in the space created between the inner contour lines of both Adam and Eve's legs, one finds them almost directly repeated in Nerdrum's painting.

In his biblical scene Masaccio had depicted God punishing the first human beings after they had eaten from the tree of knowledge and laid the foundation for what we would call a civilized society: they had, according to Genesis (3: 5-6) learnt to distinguish «good and evil» and had arrived at a notion of consciousness – «reason». An angel armed with a sword was sent down to expel them from Paradise and to send them off to a life of anxiety and uncertainty. But when Nerdrum says that the main character in *Iron Law* is «the little man who walks into a virgin landscape,» he has apparently turned this Biblical myth of original sin on its head and has driven man back to another kind of utopian paradise beyond good and evil.[15] The angel with the sword has been transformed into a man carrying a wooden stick ready to perform the painful ritual of the «iron law» on a figure who offers no resistance when subjected to the abusive treatment. These two figures form a portal or a gateway in the landscape, readily seen as a symbol of that «rite of passage» in which Nerdrum seems to rob man of the element that keeps him civilized, namely consciousness. The law thus suggests that the original unity – the natural state of man – cannot be realized unless we lose our current form of consciousness. But, as Sartre pointed out, consciousness resists the loss of itself. In order for

called it, was also clear: «When man feels betrayed by society, it is his birthright to return to a natural state.»[13]

In the painted world of Odd Nerdrum, however, it was

Masaccio: *Expulsion from Paradise,* 1426 – 28. Santa Maria del Carmine, Firenze.

24. *Iron Law*, 1983 – 84. 82 ¾ x 107 in.

his characters to have their Being in Nothingness, Ner-drum must therefore have them literally beat each other out of their minds before they can proceed into nature with the sound of eternity ringing in their ears.

While painting this «virgin» landscape, he also found a solution to the problem of how to depict the new universe his characters were to inhabit, a world as naked as their bodies and as alien as their minds. The idea of this waste-land had in fact occurred to him during a visit to the Museum of Natural History in New York in 1983, when he saw a tableau of the Russian taiga; and it had stuck in his mind as he watched Long Island spread out beneath him during a takeoff from Kennedy Airport. In *Iron Law* the horizon is so extremely curved that it makes the earth appear to have shrunk into a singular substance of soil and watcr, just as Sassctta and other medieval painters depicted their visions of the world before Renaissance man had in-vented the visual logic of a central perspective. Nerdrum was not unacquainted with this period in the history of art, but he also cites a sudden recollection of the aerial view he got of the horizon on his childhood airplane rides as a reason for introducing this type of landscape in the painting: «I simply repeated what I had seen as a child, in order to feel at home there.»[16] When in addition he lets a dramatically glowing sky spread out over his endless world, it becomes clear that he must also have had in mind «the hour of timelessness – the hour of twilight.» These fated elements combine to create a unique state of nature in the landscape, creating an archaic twilight world where the reflection of timelessness in man and nature is one and the same. This was the kingdom of a natural im-perative as seen from an eternal point of view, and very different from anything he had once found in the art of the Renaissance and the Baroque.

From this eternal point of view Nerdrum now comple-ted the transformation of his art. In *The Mother* (25) calm has descended on his archaic twilight landscape. The flight from civilization is ended, and man has fallen asleep. The blunted and rounded forms are back, and the mother en-velops her children as the animal hide does her body and the leather helmet her head. In this deserted landscape Nerdrum has given them a new security based on nature, not on culture. The world has been recreated as a mental refuge, where man obeys the same laws as nature. This is a world that, in all its rejecting bleakness, is indeed meant to be a positive place for Nerdrum's abused and beaten in-dividuals, for nature is here no longer man's adversary – it is man's salvation.

Once Nerdrum's new man reawoke in his refuge, he was subjected to his final metamorphosis – *The Trans-figuration* (26), depicted here as the transformation of the rebellious contemporary man into the true archetypal hu-man being. The Negro rises like a sphinx amidst the slee-ping bundles, staring, open-mouthed, into an Arcadian wasteland. The scene is peaceful and sublime. But what is it that he is likely to see?

In his analysis of the sublime in nature Immanuel Kant, whom Nerdrum sometimes referred to during this period, had stated that the source of our experience of na-ture's grandeur and infinity lay within ourselves, not in nature. The sublime did not lie in nature's own phenome-na, but in our minds, and only in so far as we were superi-or to nature as morally sensitive and reasoning beings. To Kant nature was «a mere nothing in comparison with the ideas of reason.»[17] But Nerdrum's intentions had, ever since *Twilight*, been the exact opposite. He wanted to em-phasize nature and the natural in man as a better guide than our rational ideas about that same nature. When he painted his landscapes and tried to elevate man by virtue of man's absolute participation in nature, it was not in or-der to affirm, but to disavow a blind faith in an enlighte-ned mind and to create a world inhabited by individuals functioning radically different from common norms.

According to himself, his intention was to establish an isolated world with no contact with our own, since: «My pictures do not relate to society, only to themselves. They are introverted. The landscapes and characters seek no contact with you. You stand outside, looking in at this world as through a keyhole. They do not know of your existence, and they are also indifferent to you because they are living their own lives.»[18]

The question of what the transfigured individual is likely to see with his dreamy look is a question of what ontological status Nerdrum may have given his figures when he established his enclosed world. If we were to walk around as gaping dreamers, we would scarcely function as cogs in the social machinery, being instead relegated to the role of maladjusted «idiots.» And it was precisely this kind

25. *The Mother, 1985 – 1994.* 59 ½ x 69 in.

of deranged or functionally demented outsider that interested Nerdrum and formed his symbolic gateway to the
mentality that reigned within his refuge. In *The Ultimate
Sight* (27) we find three of them surveying a misty waste-
land with a «fool's look of astonishment,» as though whatever they might be seeing is being seen with eyes very different from our own.[19] The atmosphere of the painting
has some of the same wistful uncertainty that Nerdrum
had captured in *The Seabird* (2). In this case, however, the
spectator might also feel uncertain, for what takes place in
front of the strange characters seems to mean something
different to them than to us. We perceive only emptiness
and bleakness in this sublime infinity, while they seem
filled with a presence that almost makes them part of their
own view. The interrelationship of man and nature in *The
Ultimate Sight* is thus of a purely physical, not a metaphysical, kind. These beings seem to exist as nature within
nature, not reflecting on why they are not masters of it.
They are what they see, not what they think, having
already entered a world we can only long for.

In this painting Nerdrum had used a number of props
that recall Brueghel's blind beggars and village idiots, and
especially the Middle Ages. At first sight it also seems as if
he has used this kind of imagery in his *Portrait of Arild
Haaland* (28), painted as a blind prophet entranced in the
sort of spiritual ecstasy that divine revelation might evoke
in the elders in Gothic depictions of the apocalypse. This
is, however, only at first sight. Here, as in *The Ultimate
Sight*, the references to this period are better seen as a
means rather than an end. Nor do the leather bands
around his head and the furry cloak covering his body
support the association of this prophetic figure with the
Middle Ages. Nerdrum himself claims to have given his
model «a timeless costume, like a kind of prehistoric philosopher.»[20] And the obvious anachronism of tying prehistoric man to a rationally motivated advocate of ideas –
including his remote expression – provides a decisive clue
as to where in history Nerdrum sought out his affinities.

Although Haaland is a philosopher, Nerdrum did not
portray him as one. When the first philosophers appeared
in Greece in the seventh century B.C., they certainly did
not stand gawking at the sky. The philosophers were like
us, searching for rational explanations, rules of logic, and
systems within the concepts they had developed to better

understand their new psychology and the nature they observed. The character in the painting does, however, bear
some resemblance to the biblical prophets of the Old
Testament from about the eighth to the sixth century B.C.
These prophets, who were called *nabiim* in Hebrew, had
the ability, independently of any force of will, to enter a
state described by the verb *naba*. This meant to call forth
God in a state of prophetic ecstasy.[21] In addition to Isaiah
and Jeremiah, Amos is the most typical example. He was
an illiterate shepherd who continually received messages
through the voice of God or by seeing him in visions. He
recites the content of what he «sees» and «hears» wherever
he happens to be, giving no thought to the message before
delivering it. The first book of Samuel (10:3-13) has an
account of Saul's meeting a whole company of these
*nabiim* wandering around in the wilderness prophesying.
These roaming prophets are also described in other
sources and are commonly known, along with the Greek
oracles and other illiterate ecstatics, until the fifth century
B.C., when there is a dramatic change. From now on the
prophets mentioned in the Bible are teachers of morality
equipped with a normal consciousness, or, as in the case of
the Preacher, a sceptical philosopher, who, like his Greek
counterparts, reflects upon the feeling that «all is vani-
ty…I turned my mind to know and to search out and to
seek wisdom and the sum of things, and to know the
wickedness of folly and the foolishness which is mad-
ness.»[22] By now the pre-conscious prophet's conduct has
become so wicked, foolish, and mad that Zechariah pre-
scribes the death penalty for anyone still going about
prophesying: «And if anyone again appears as a prophet,
his mother and father who bore him will say to him, 'You
shall not live, for You speak lies in the name of the Lord':
and his father and mother who bore him shall pierce him
through when he prophesies. And on that day every prophet will be ashamed of his vision, when he prophesies; he
will not put on a hairy mantle in order to deceive . . .»[23]

It is quite clear that Nerdrum makes use of his «hairy-
mantled» prophet much as he did when he turned the
Christian mythology of the rise of consciousness upside
down in his *Iron Law*, reversing the mental evolution
shown in the Bible towards times far closer to that «starting point» or «state of nature» where man was not yet
estranged from the nature within himself. The blinded

**26.** *The Transfiguration,* 1984 – 1997. 69 ½ x 98 ¾ in.

27. *The Ultimate Sight,* 1985 – 1992. 46 ½ x 57 ½ in.

28. *Portrait of Arild Haaland,* 1984. 37 x 32 in.

appearance given Haaland may also be an indication of this, since the ancient Greeks often associated this handicap with such extraordinary mental powers as those held by their poets. In the oldest parts of the *Iliad*, from the thirteenth century B.C. the strange and cruel heroes are driven not by the consciousness of self that later guided Ulysses, but by a host of hallucinated gods. This was also the case with the poets, or bards, who sang, rather than read, forth the story of this epos, before Homer assured its written recording several centuries later. The singers of the *Iliad* were under the direct hallucinatory influence of some godlike beings they called muses. These were the daughters of Mnemosyne, whose name was later turned into the term *memory* by the more civilized Greeks. Unlike the poets of our acquaintance, the first bards did not compose their verses in advance, but instead «experienced» the story directly and sang it spontaneously. There is such a bard also in the *Odyssey*, but he is already there an aberration. Ulysses asks him to sing of Ulysses' own experiences in Troy, of which the bard could have no knowledge. Suddenly, reports Homer, «a god commanded him to begin his song.»[24] Ulysses verified the tale that welled forth from the singer by bursting into tears. The bard's name was Demodocus, and, just like Haaland in Nerdrum's portrayal – and Homer himself – he was blind, for the muses had «robbed him of his eyes, but lending sweetness to his song.»[25] This is the first time that the idiosyncrasies peculiar to the pre-conscious human mind are described as a compensation for a physical handicap. And looking at another couple of paintings that were part of the mental redefinition Nerdrum's figures were subjected to at this time, we find this compensatory idea repeated. This is true of both *The One-Armed Aviator* (29) and the crippled *Night Guard* (30), paintings he made the drawings for just after the Haaland portrait in 1984.

Just as might be suspected when looking at paintings such as *Iron Law* and *Man in Abandoned Landscape*, the image of *The One-Armed Aviator* is probably meant to be one of Nerdrum himself. Here the victimized amputee lifts his gaze to the dark, stormy sky. On the horizon there is a threatening, beak-shaped cloud. It is not clear, however, whether he fears or longs for these forces of upheaval, but since misfortune seems inevitable, as it had been to the helmsman of the boatload of refugees, the association

of the darkened sky with Nerdrum's relationship to his legal father seems close at hand. The black leather helmet, which also covers the head of the uncommunicatively gaping *Night Guard*, is, however, an attribute of a more general significance. The helmet was taken from Nerdrum's vivid childhood image of a mentally retarded messenger boy riding a moped. And it was in reference to the status given to such mentally deficient and outcast individuals in our society that he commented on the appearance of his figures at the time: «the weak individual is the salvation of mankind. The aberrant is the night guard of the world.»[66] In our acceptance of the conditions laid down by a rational age we were the real idiots. And since Nerdrum had so clearly indicated that he was among those who would acquiesce no more, he probably pictured himself as the one being on guard while others slept.

Nerdrum also strove to achieve a basic, archetypal quality in the use of signifying elements in his compositions. The night guard has been surrounded by the peaceful sleepers as a collection of unidentifiable, bundled bodies, swaddled in animal hides and natural fabrics. Only the foreground figures stand out with their feet almost protruding from the canvas, creating the strong impression of tangible physical presence, so typical of Nerdrum's paintings. The group as a whole is also formed into an archetypal sign. The guard, who turns to his symbolic source of light in the early dawn, is enclosed in the circle formed by the sleepers around him – a shape repeated in the circular cloud on the right. This circular and physically protective enclosure of the main character is also the theme in *Revier* (31) – a personal territory where the bald, elderly wanderer has built a little stony refuge of his own in the desert. One foot has a primitive shoe strapped to it, as a sign that he still has one leg in our own time; and the rocks are placed in the same sort of formation created by stone-age inhabitants in Britain in their construction of Stonehenge 1700 B.C. The form is here more likely an expression of Nerdrum's desire for a secluded personal territory than of a kind of archaic sun worship, although that is not out of the question. In *Return of the Sun* (32) this is precisely what he shows, by having the three young women reach out towards the sun's life-giving rays in «prophetic ecstasy.» Here the ecstatic women seem to have entered into a purely physical relationship with the sun, as

**29.** *The One-Armed Aviator,* 1987. 45 ½ x 35 ¼ in.

**30.** *The Night Guard,* 1986 – 1998. 80 ¾ x 98 ½ in.

**31.** *Revier,* 1986 – 1998. 51 ½ x 63 in.

These forms are also repeated in *Return of the Sun*, especially in the lower of the circular clouds and in the little fingers of the nearly identical twin sisters. Nerdrum deliberately gave these twins some of the finer features from Munch's *Sick Child* (fig.), not only because his beloved pupil, and model for the *Anine* painting, resembled her more than did his model for *Isola*, Trine Folmoe, but because he felt that Munch had here managed to convey that look of timeless beauty that he himself sought to recreate, and which he had recognized in the related *Jacob Blessing the Sons of Joseph* by Rembrandt (fig.). Should the eye wander, however, and notice the white T-shirts, there is no longer any trace of timeless beauty. Nor was there meant to be.

All of the modern props in the pictures he painted at this time were intended as reminders that the people now inhabiting his world had newly arrived from ours, and that they had not simply moved backwards in time. In terms of mentality there was clearly a question of a symbolic retreat to more archaic forms; but the arena of their lives, or the venue where they acted out their new nature, was apparently independent of any particular era. This becomes clear in a painting such as *The Memory Hall* (34), where Nerdrum has portrayed himself contemplating an architectural form which is not archeological in our sense, but which instead seems to date back to our time as seen from a distant future. Still, this dating has an element of uncertainty. In 1984 Nerdrum spoke of his characters as having entered a «prehistoric existence,» while he claimed that the paintings had a «post-historic look.» [27] The immediate confusion disappears, however, when it turns out that this «post-historic» carries no vision of the future in a linear sense, but is meant to be a truly «timeless,» fictional state in which history has ceased to exist and where the memory hall can be seen as the timeless man's memory of time itself.

When he exhibited this painting in 1986, together with the first versions of a couple of related works, such as *The Water Protectors* (35) and *The Cloud* (36), many critics saw them as actual descriptions of the future. Nerdrum refuted the idea that his technological ruins and modern attributes were meant to convey a vision of the post-nuclear society. His concern was «not with what things would look like after a possible nuclear disaster. Dates, for example, do not exist in this world, because it has nothing to do with the

Nerdrum has made it the source of the vital energy that fills them once they emerge from the cold and blinding darkness of civilization. As in the other outsider pictures this also seems to focus on man's reentry into the perennial cycle of nature, where the cyclical turning of the sun has resumed its reign over the linear way of thinking that it once had among the Egyptians, as referred to in *Isola*.

These types of blind female figures, reflecting the colors of the sky in their empty eyes, were a motif that had appeared in the first version of the blue *Isola* (33) in 1984. In this second version, with its Hertervig-influenced cloud formations, Nerdrum has introduced a number of repetitive details, for instance the constantly repeated hook shapes.

Edvard Munch: *Sick Child*, 1885–1886. Nasjonalgalleriet, Oslo.
Rembrandt: *Jacob Blessing the Sons of Joseph*, Gemäldegalerie, Kassel.

**32.** *Return of the Sun,* 1986 – 1995. 41 ¾ x 63 ½ in.

**33.** *Isola,* 1987. 25 ½ x 32 ¼ in.

34. *The Memory Hall*, 1985. 45 x 47 in.

**35.** *The Water Protectors,* 1985 – 1993. 98 ½ x 80 ¾ in.

36. *The Cloud,* 1985 – 1993. 48 ½ x 54 ½ in.

linear way of thinking in our civilization. Time has dissolved into an eternity with no beginning and no end. Thus I can use whatever I want when it comes to garments and weapons. But these people have to carry guns in order to protect themselves against those living in our world. For we are the ones who constitute the greatest threat to their autonomy and spiritual existence. So, you see, it's all on a mental level.»[28]

Nerdrum also dismissed the notion that the dark, heavy clouds that had now begun to appear in his paintings were loaded with radioactive fallout. The shark-like shape of *The Cloud* had, in other words, nothing to do with our nuclear technology, although it was a sign of some form of menace or evil, as other iconographic elements in the painting could also be seen – for instance the little hammer-shaped cloud to the left and the small pond in the landscape, which is reminiscent of a wolf's eye. On the top right of the cloud lies the lion of courage, forming a positive sign in the picture.[29] These signs are, however, more likely to be directed at us than at the man bent over the oval omphalus rock in the middle of the refuge. Nerdrum is an animist when painting his landscape; but here it is not animated by any higher spirituality in us. The man studying these elements encounters only other forms of natural substances than the one represented by himself: «My man,» says Nerdrum, «is like a dog that has discovered something and fearlessly pursues what it sees. Both he, the cloud, and the landscape live their own lives. I merely confront them with one another as independent entities.»[30] It was important to Nerdrum to point out how his people differed mentally from what one might expect in such a situation, that he later wrote of the character in *The Cloud*: «This is a man who has lost all words and has a wordless conversation with the cloud,» adding: «The people I have depicted have become less and less tied to our concept of security. They exist in a greater world than our own. They have neither an overview nor the upper hand, for all that surrounds them is nameless. What our world has relieved us of is what they live in. They seek different answers.»[31]

A picture like *The Water Protectors* (35) also illustrates how Nerdrum's paintings take on a whole new meaning when his nameless world is seen as one fundamentally different from our own. Viewed in a linear view of the future, as was common among critics in the eighties, these people

become rational builders of a civilization just as we are, or survival machines like the *Mad Max* character from George Miller's movies.[32] The three figures will then have a normal social function, either by defending their water supply or by making sure that no one drinks polluted water. But Nerdrum obviously had other intentions. It may thus well be a reflection of the «natural state» he was trying to depict that is found in the strange eyes of the middle water protector. The peculiarly beautiful face has an expression as open as that of the Egyptian *Isola*, but also as distant and unapproachable. And just like Nerdrum's favorite author of his youth, Dostoyevsky, had portrayed his naive Count Myshkin in *The Idiot*, Nerdrum seems to have depicted his character as, if anything, even more liberated from the sham of reason and the greed of desire. He must have given him the task of defending the water of life; and all we know for certain that he «knows,» is that he does not want to be like us again. He has gone into an inner exile.

Reflecting on his project, Nerdrum admitted there was a degree of normalcy to his general desire for escape: «It may also be typical of our time to establish a kind of inner existence, a spare lung for breathing, which makes everything all right even when things are all wrong.» But behind this desire lay perhaps a more atypical need to express a highly personal, if not directly private dimension on the canvas, since Nerdrum added to his analysis that «modern man seems to have lost his ability to concentrate. He breaks his attendance in life into fragments of entertainment. But I have not entered this world in order to be entertained. I have come to have my life confirmed.»[33] Evidence of this can be found in his self-portrait *Man with a Leather Helmet* (37), where the headgear definitely does not cover a dumb fool. His gaze is neutral, but the posture is very self-assertive, as he stands elevated far above the clouds, virtually assuming the role of Thor in Norse mythology. The first title he used for this motif, in 1985, was *Warrior*, a term that seemed more in keeping with his self-image as an old master general in a hostile art world, while his own description of his position was: «All my life I have been a lonely hunter in a wilderness.»[34] And in *The Memory Hall* the heroic role he has given himself is even more obvious, for here Hercules' club has been replaced by a gun, and the puma's hide is nothing but a trophy.

In *Man with Seeds* (38) he has positioned himself in

37. *Man with a Leather Helmet,* 1985 – 1995. 34 ¼ x 28 ¾ in.

front of a large bank of earth at night. And yet the light is so strong that he is forced to squint. In one hand he holds a spade. In the other lie thirteen fateful seeds. He is obviously trying to show us something, for his gesture is directed at us, who are outside his world. Nerdrum is very reticent and reserved when asked about the intentions behind his various motifs, but he does say that his basic ideas are visions coming from a personally local, idiosyncratic level, and then launched into a universal sphere: «Initially the idea appears as a sensory image, which I put into a context where it becomes humanized. The ideas are often insane visions that I go on to put into a human context . . . When I start working, there is often some local meanness in the picture; but as I keep on working, I force it out of the local towards an eternal, universal image – a transformation.»[35] This means that what might have had a strictly private origin will appear to us as universal symbols with which we can identify and which we can recognize as either mythical or archetypal in nature. This is also true of the thirteen seeds to be sown. The significance of his gesture may on a universal level point to a form of his generally sacralizing approach to man's basic bodily needs, in a world where nature itself could also appear in its most crude and basic form. It is as if he has dug a hole in the Mother Earth archetype of C.G. Jung, about to sow the fresh seeds of life, since they have always found their best conditions for growth in the warm, dark, and moist cavities of nature. And it is quite possible that such an act was also the concrete and purely private source of the symbolic code invested in this imagery.

In Nerdrum's earlier landscapes the symbolism of natural openings had only appeared in *Man in Abandoned Landscape* (23). But in the spring of 1986, after his return from his first of many visits to Iceland, he began painting natural forms clearly inspired by the earth and sulphur-colored lava mountains of this volcanic island, where the holes that allowed for a direct interaction of the basic elements of earth, air, fire, and water were well represented. In *Sleeping Courier* (39), his first Icelandic landscape, the caves and holes have less to do with our ancestors' dwellings than with «Gaia's» organic metabolism. Seen from the eternal point of view of nature itself, the protective cocoon shape he has given the *Sleeping Courier* may refer to the budding life's shielding of itself. The resemblance of

the wrapped figure to a mummy may also evoke associations with death, as an integral part of nature's cyclical processes. The courier's «task» in Nerdrum's universe is therefore not unequivocal, especially when the threatening look of the darkish woman in *Armed Woman* (40), initially called *Armed Courier*, indicates that it is our own world she is in contact with. It is thus possible that Nerdrum pictured the sleeping woman as a messenger coming from the outside world into his own isolated enclosure, and that only in this world, by virtue of her symbolic iconography, including her form, which fits the shape of the hole leading to the underground, she has been given the task of both representing and communicating between life and death. For death was not an unknown phenomenon in this world. It was present as the flip side of life.

In *Sole Morte* (41), or «Lonely Death,» one of the inhabitants of the refuge has just exhaled his last breath into the water that is the very intermediary between life and death in traditional symbolism. This man has ended his life, apparently fearlessly reconciled with the inevitability of death. On his face, which is reflected, or rather doubled in the surface of the water, there is less evidence of the death of Narcissus than of a man who has lived his life according to his own nature and now leaves it in the same way. When asked about his motif, Nerdrum found it necessary to stress its relationship to Greek mythology: «I have painted the youth, the one that existed before Narcissus . . . What existed before the myth, what took place earlier . . . Everything I do is a deconstruction and then a reconstruction.»[36] In no version of the myth does Narcissus drown in the water he uses as a mirror, but in one of them he has a past that allows for a metaphoric connection to the painting. For the beautiful Narcissus had a twin sister who was his exact counterpart in every way, even a soul mate – in Nerdrum's terms: a twin soul. When she died and he could no longer see himself in her, his grief was so profound that he had to recall her existence in his own mirror image. He pined away lovesick over a life he was himself a part of.[37]

The strange, elliptical cloud Nerdrum had included as a sign of death in *Sole Morte* first appeared in the 1986 *Black Cloud* (42). That was also the first time the characters populating his Icelandic lava landscape were shown as a couple in a shared territory – despite the fact that only

38. *Man with Seeds,* 1986 – 1992. 52 ½ x 43 ¾ in.

**39.** *Sleeping Courier,* 1986 – 1996. 66 x 76 ¾ in.

40. *Armed Woman,* 1986 – 1993. 33 x 28 in.

**42.** *The Black Cloud,* 1986. 62 ½ x 76 ¾ in.

**41.** *Sole Morte,* 1987 – 1993. 69 ¾ x 77 ½ in.

one of them was a real nomad, judging by the single wanderer's staff. The woman, whom we recognize from *Sleeping Courier*, stares vacantly up at the sky, baring her breasts. The man is equally exposed, as he has dislodged one arm from the unified body and engaged in a «wordless conversation» with the ominous cloud. His index finger is bent inwards and points towards the woman. If Nerdrum is right in a comment made shortly after having completed the painting – that what happens in his world expresses «the essence of life and the primality of things»[38] – it is not very helpful as a guide to understanding his more personal motivations. But in *Sleeping Twins* (43), where the *Anine* model for the third time lies down on the lava ground, the signs are clearer. In «this symbiosis between nature and longing,» as he would later describe this motif, she is portrayed in a double edition, just as he made the face of the dead man in *Sole Morte* double itself in the water.[39] In addition he makes sleep, this state full of possibilities somewhere between life and death, into a theme in this plain and beautiful painting, where the contours of an advanced pregnancy reveal growing life-forms beneath the delicately painted animal hides. Significantly enough Nerdrum has once again, as he had in *Amputation*, lifted his viewpoint off the ground in order to have the spectator hover above the fertile twins as if he were an alien bird. For when he again used his pupil as a model, it was in the role of a *Woman with Milk* (44), who, eyes downcast, displays to the two deferential women the water of life in another consistency. However, Nerdrum did not only paint what he saw in his model; he has also painted something he imagined. She never bore a child, nor did she ever show any sign of pregnancy.

The method of deconstruction/reconstruction – which corresponds to Derrida's philosophy – that Nerdrum employed in order to universalize the topical content of his paintings he also used on his forms. In *Sole Morte* all elements are still recognizable as nature, but the naturalistically painted landscape illusion has become secondary. Instead the various elements in the painting rest on their expressiveness as forms and are subordinated to the totality. Even the technical «mistakes» are intentional. The huge rock formation rises like a flat wall, repeating the shape of the dead man, while the simple cloud makes up for what it lacks in plasticity by its pregnancy as signifier, a shape that

is repeated in the puddle and in the piece of cloth on the ground. The same relationships can be seen in *The Black Cloud*, where the nominally naturalistic cloud's elliptical and «substantial natural shape» is repeated in various parts of the composition. Nerdrum describes these sign entities, with their slowly moving patterns, as «plain, archetypal forms;» and he feels that they «lie like a primordial awareness in man.»[40] They can be found throughout his compositions, since he wants the separate elements of a picture not only to rest securely within themselves, but also to resemble one another, in order to achieve an internal dialogue. «With a style like mine,» he explained in reference to the origin of these characteristic features in his paintings, «it is not a matter of inventing anything, but just revealing your inner ornamentation.»[41]

This ornamentation also revealed a strong urge towards orderly compositions on Nerdrum's part. In *Sleeping Twins* the figures lay like abstract signs forming two vertical columns, symmetrically placed and harmoniously balanced both in relationship to one another and to the dark, diffuse background. It is probably the closest Nerdrum has ever come to the «pure forms» of modernism, although this was not where he was headed. His aim was rather the sacralizing function of the symmetrical composition, which by now had become a recurring feature in his work. In *The Seed Protectors* (45) he has also locationally elevated his triangular scene up onto a cult-like assembly ground high up in a mountainous Icelandic landscape. Although Nerdrum's inspiration often came from very specific locations in Iceland, he rarely allowed naturalism enough room to make them recognizable. Sometimes his art-historical eclecticism might result in ties to entirely different landscapes than the Icelandic one, as seen, for example, in the strictly symmetrical and ornamental *Man against Open Sky* (46), in which it is instead the vista from Leonardo's *Mona Lisa* that has made its way behind the encapsulated power kit placed between the twin clouds. The reason why Nerdrum's encounter with the Icelandic landscape was a revelation on par with Rembrandt in Stockholm and Caravaggio in Rome, was that it appeared as new-born, naked, and barren as he wanted man to appear in his painted world. It is this kind of mental nakedness that characterizes the three throning, almost iconic figures in *The Seed Protectors*. Despite being neutrally expressionless and dis-

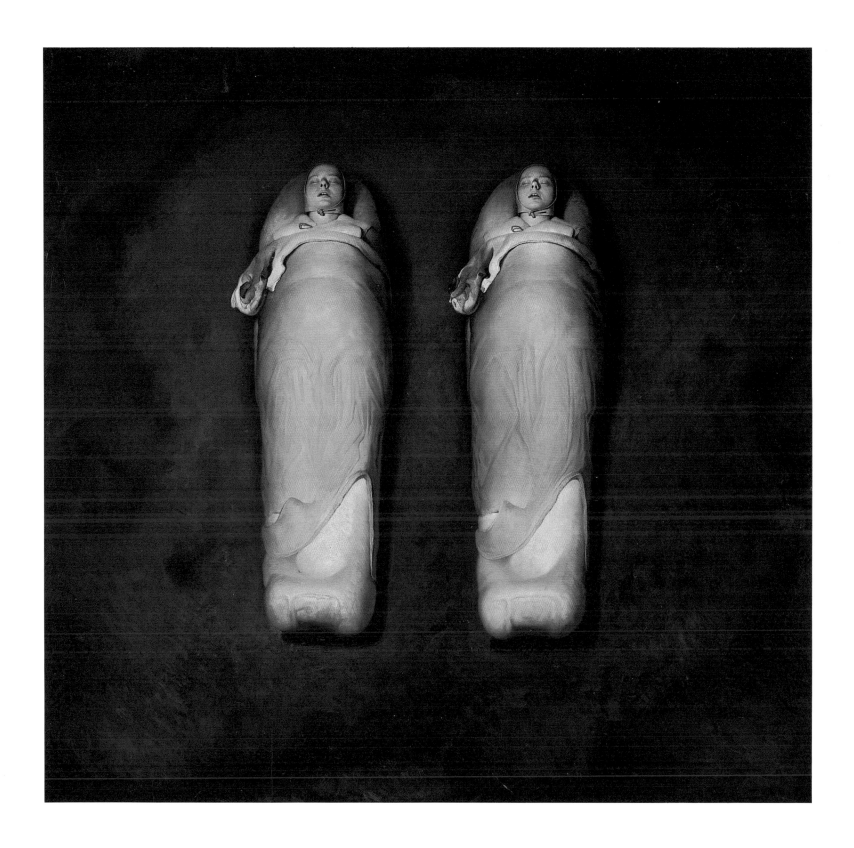

43. *Sleeping Twins*, 1987.  98  x 96 ½ in.

**45.** *The Seed Protectors,* 1987 – 1996. 63 ¾ x 76 ¾ in.

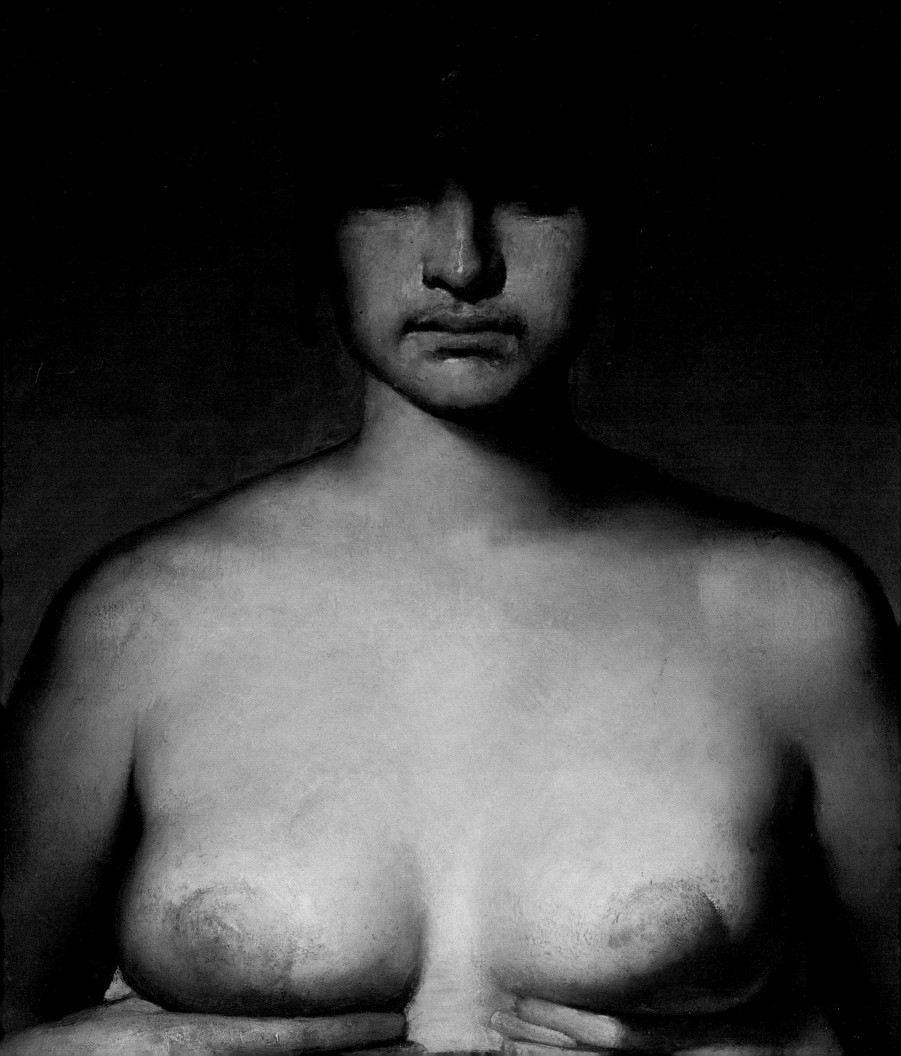

44. *Woman with Milk*, 1988 – 1993. 92 ½ x 82 ¾ in.

tantly indifferent, they radiate an innocent sincerity and a stoic dignity, which Nerdrum is far from alone in associating with a «natural state» in man. But the fateful gravity one senses in this painting is not only based on the body language and gestures of the figures. The man with his back bare kneeling in the foreground has assumed a subservient posture and has subjected himself to their bidding. They have something he needs and are therefore given the power to decide his fate. A social hierarchy has been established in the refuge. The psychological mood of the painting is thus more likely to evoke thoughts of the insensitive roughness displayed in the Icelandic sagas – stories Nerdrum loved and devoured during this period – than to Thomas Moore's fairyland *Utopia*, which he occasionally mentioned. But this remote and hostile world was his own creation, not a product of anyone else's imagination. And as this was the place where he lived out his visions, the answer to what the pictures contained must be sought in that direction. For only he who has knowledge of the essence can tell when appearances are deceptive.

The extent to which Nerdrum's depiction of social hierarchies coincides with other views of man's true nature is not as important as his explicit aim of portraying his characters as «timeless, classless, and genderless.»[42] This raises questions concerning a picture such as *Woman with Milk*, in which the unmistakable ranking order is based on her gender-determined pregnancy. But Nerdrum did not support modernity's dissolution of individual and social differences, its destruction of traditional sex roles, and above all its total focusing on the present. This was not only because he found it very refreshing to contradict the politically correct masses. He wanted to penetrate the «noble» facades and the «sincerely felt» banalities, to get at what he called «the bounds of necessity in life,»[43] within which he could pay tribute to this woman as the life-giving principle in nature. Within these bounds her value is entirely based on her ability to act in accordance with her biological nature – not, as in our culture, on her capacity for earning professional titles. In this context the woman's role in maintaining our civilization's forms of thought and production is as irrelevant as the man's, for here we are all equally far removed from the «starting point» Nerdrum wanted man restored to. On a universal level the theme of this painting is man's capacity for grasping the most pro-

found reason for his existence as a species, rather than his shortcoming in breaking down or undermining this existence. «The most important thing,» he explained, «is to make people see that nearly everything we now look upon as qualities are negations of the true qualities.»[44] Nerdrum's objective was to represent all «that man has abandoned in order to make the world go around the way it does.»[45] In this sense his entire archaic utopia was a counter-image, in which he reflected all that we are not, in order to show who we really are.

By painting these timeless scenes – carefully processed by using durable natural materials in a time when art has become invaded by technology and characterized by transitoriness – Nerdrum also exemplified some of the qualities sacrificed along the road to our current social machinery. For he has always regarded the craftsmanship invested in his paintings to be of major importance. If a picture was not well painted, it would simply be lost in the multitude of visual pollution. Even his own ideas and thematic references ran the risk of becoming outdated and uninteresting. Then it would not matter that he had said something significant about man, the world, or himself, if it were not conveyed in an interesting way. Only the skillful execution of a painting could ensure its survival. What mattered was the quality of the painted surfaces rendering flesh, fabric, and other materials through which nature and the genuinely human could be communicated. And although very few artists could match his skills by the eighties, his ambitions in terms of techniques and brushwork have continued to spur him on in his search for painterly beauty and visual power.

In Nerdrum's characteristic use of shapes and forms – faintly related to Blake's organic rhythmics, to icon painting, and to elements in the symbolist Ferdinand Hodler's compositions – the old masters had remained in the background. But not in terms of craftsmanship. The techniques used by Rembrandt in his later years had always fascinated him – even to the extent that he recognized details of the clothing in *The Jewish Bride* in the sulphurous mountains of Iceland. Another master who would become ever more important to him was Titian, especially the way he painted towards the end of his life. In his earlier paintings Nerdrum had rarely painted flesh and other important areas exclusively by the use of local colors. There is an

**46.** *Man against Open Sky*, 1988 – 1990. 43 ¾ x 46 in.

increasing frequency now, however, of the short strokes and dabs of paint he incorporates and uses in making up the larger areas. This was a method Titian began using when he embarked on his «ultima maniera,» later taken to its peak in his rough «spot painting.» In the late eighties, Nerdrum apparently starts to employ Titian's various techniques in different ways in one and the same painting. Less important areas, such as parts of the landscape and lower edges of the composition are often so roughly executed that the contours of the shapes become blurred, while crucial parts, such as the face of *Woman with Milk*, are made up of a range of color tones arranged in small fields or simply with short, gentle brushstrokes. The colors are generally mixed or contrasted with warm gray, «the mother of all colors,» as Nerdrum calls it – juxtaposing red and yellow to green and blue, in order to give a glow to cool areas and tone down warm ones. This is, however, not a question of an impressionist exercise. The colors are there to render surfaces and textures as convincingly as possible, or to in themselves act as metaphors for different natural substances, as in Nerdrum's favorite brown – «a mix of excrement, blood, and flesh.»[46] He usually finishes the more meticulously worked parts of the painting by layer upon layer of glaze and fresh new strokes. In some of the more extensive areas of flesh he also sometimes uses another technique, letting the fan-shaped blender soften the transition between the flesh tones and form new lines in the wet paint using crossing strokes. As often as not, Nerdrum scrapes away the day's work, starting afresh in new attempts to unify the forms and give life to the textures. His self-scrutiny and demand for quality in the finished product some-times keep him working for months on a single painting. Despite his experience and hard work he is thus unable to exceed five or six major paintings a year. When he manages to complete only one painting some years, such as in 1989, it is because he works on several compositions simultaneously, finishing them only when they are to be exhibited. That particular year, however, there may also have been other, more personally distressing reasons.

Throughout the eighties Nerdrum had made use of his calm, «inner» ornamental forms to create relatively harmonious scenes. Although some of the paintings have exalted characters, as *The Night Guard* and the three women in *Return of the Sun*, this seems to have been more of an ex-pression of relief than of an inner tension and dissonance. In two of the paintings he made in 1988, however, both the physical drama and the psychological charge had evidently increased in the nomadic figures that inhabited his refuge. *The Storyteller* (47) has left his dark cave and tossed a burning branch on the ground. In a desperate effort to communicate his silent message he has, for one brief, intense moment, left the earth to which he belongs. The armed spectator stands stiff-necked and self-protective in a pose reminiscent of *Isola*, looking disbelievingly at the jumper. Perhaps he understands no more than we do of the message that virtually explodes in the body of the naked cave-dweller. It is not easy to see what Nerdrum may have meant by telling a story about a storyteller; but in light of his interviews that year it seems that his general criticism of our civilization was now reaching its peak.[47] From this perspective he may be seen to have used the explosive figure to point to the destructive role rational man has played in natural history, in which our short-lived, energy-consuming, technological culture has depleted global resources, requiring a return to basics if our species is to survive. But in this case it is more likely that *The Storyteller* actually represents Nerdrum himself – who that very year announced that he had not entered this world for the purpose of being entertained, but to have his life confirmed.

If so, Nerdrum has illustrated his own dilemma – that he as a narrative painter could not reveal the actual story he was telling. Immediately before he began working on the painting he had stated: «My art is something they (the audience) must confront, cracking a few codes of their own, only to get a blow they will definitely not appreciate.» But he was unwilling to disclose any of these codes: «To me it is bad enough having to find titles for my pictures. If I were to say something about them in addition, it would be seen as laying down the law, ruling out other possible interpretations on the part of critics and art historians.»[48] There is, however, reason to suspect that he was not altogether comfortable remaining silent about what he could not speak. His very reason for painting these subjects lay precisely in their deepest and most private layers of meaning, since only there could he find confirmation of his life. He had sought, by means of a range of signs and symbols, to tell his wordless story of persons and circumstances that he himself had made nameless in the paint-

47. *The Storyteller,* 1988. 76 x 114 ¼ in.

ings, but which undoubtedly had their names in his own mind. His outspoken criticism of society and all the mythical references in his pictures simply worked as a camouflage. Neither critics nor more inquisitive observers like myself saw through the cover-up and went beneath the surface. For when Nerdrum painted *The Storyteller*, in early 1988, I was writing the first book that attempted an interpretation of his eighties work[49] – on a universal level, not on a private one. Seen in this light, it is quite possible that the frustrated and irate *Storyteller* is an indicator of all the silent hints he had tried in vain to convey about the personal significance of the paintings. The reluctant spectator cannot, or will not, understand the story he is trying to tell. He is preoccupied with his own. Or, in the words by Oscar Wilde that introduced my book:

*All art is at once surface and symbol.*
*Those who go beneath the surface do so at their peril.*
*Those who read the symbol do so at their peril.*
*It is the spectator, and not life, that art really mirrors.*[50]

Odd Nerdrum would most likely heartily disagree, for his art reflects his life and no one else's.

A heart-rendering story also seems to escape from the throats of the three synchronously moving *Singers* (48), who release their inner tension through wide-open mouths in what resembles a primal scream of mankind. The presence of something unsettling is palpable, for the screamers' affected body language is not unlike that of the mythical Hippomenes, as he frantically raced to outrun the fatal Atalanta in Guido Reni's painted version, which was Nerdrum's source of inspiration for this type of figure (fig.). The pointed heap of sand that appeared both in *Man against Open Sky* and *The Storyteller* dominates the landscape with its symmetrical formation. The tensed legs

with their bent toes are outlined against the pitch-black lava, creating acute angles in a harsh, geometric use of lines. The shapes used in the 1989 *Man in Sunset* (49), in which the heap of sand has become a right-angled lava mountain, are equally harsh and painful. The figure has a wound running along his temple, and on the opposite side a triangular cloud points like a sharp wedge against his bare skull. There are no sweet sounds to be heard from his throat, either.

The tripled figure in *The Singers* was uncharacteristic of Nerdrum. When he had painted identical characters before, they had never been more than two. It is thus interesting to look at a related painting, such as *Dawn* (50), from 1990, in which the serial repetition numbers four identical figures and several mountains and clouds rhythmically repeated in the background, almost like a piece of music by Philip Glass. The frozen nomads are sitting half-naked at right angles, shielding their upper torsos with black cloaks, in an almost desperate longing to let the sun's first rays warm their bodies. They may be singing the praise of the sunrise or breathing its life-giving energy into their craving lungs, simply because «our time lacks sunrises,» as Nerdrum put it in an aphorism.[51] So did his own life at that time, at least judging by the pain and anguish he has put into *Wanderer Imitating a Cloud* (51), where the embryonic cloud from *Dawn* turns up in a single, dark version. Nerdrum has indicated that this motif may be seen as a self-portrait in which he represents «the outsider, the Jew, who remains excluded,» or «the eternal Jew,» who must forever adapt and submit to new «clouds» in life, even the most malevolent.[52] His cloth is blood red and his sleeping pad as black as his curly hair. As on the bearded Claudius Civilis one eye has been injured, and the pained look indicates that he will not be able to hold the strained semi-fetal position much longer. Only by turning the painting upside-down will the viewer realize just how long and effective legs this umbroped of a wanderer really has for walking – once he gets on his feet.

By now the tension in Nerdrum's imagery had reached a level where he himself could no longer refrain from commenting on it: «In the painting *Woman with a Door Handle* (52) there is a conflict between her hand and the metal of the handle, a stylistic incongruity rhythmically repeated throughout the picture. There are conflicting

Guido Reni: *Hippomenes and Atalanta*, 1612. Prado, Madrid.

**48.** *The Singers,* 1987 – 1988. 76 x 97 in.

**51.** *Wanderer Imitating a Cloud,* 1990. 90 ¼ x 77 ¾ in.

**49.** *Man in Sunset,* 1989. 43 ¼ x 37 ½ in.

situations, such as the evening sun on one side of the picture and a thunderstorm on the other, and the mountain behind the girl is in the shape of an animal. I have thus intentionally added intrigue in the composition, repeating the look on the girl's face, in which one eye is askew. This dark eye. I find this conflict between two concepts interesting . . . I want a painting to be at once breathtakingly beautiful and ugly.»[53] Nerdrum considers this work, with its heavily reworked and coded natural forms, as important to his new method of constructing his images as *Iron Law* had been to his landscapes. About 1990 his love of «intriguing» composition may, however, have gone a bit too far in its visual rhetoric, which he has admitted that it may have done in *Idiota* (53). The contrasts between the soft, rounded forms in the warm foreground and the cold, pointed peaks in the background are extreme. The woman's silhouette diagonally intersects the broken-up center line, and a bit to the left of the mid-axis, starting from her shoulder, a tripodal set of lines spreads along the arms and the edge of the fur. Her hands have a menacing form resembling claws, making it reasonable to interpret her closed eyes and open mouth as a sign of hostility. Her name could easily be read as of Latin origin, indicating a deficient mind or a novice. But Nerdrum is of a different opinion: «Idiota is Greek and means homey, the familiar, what is close.»[54] The embers in the fire and her large, nursing breast can thus be seen as a reference to his own domestic sphere. The curved rock formation in the background, which resembles Arnold Böcklin's *Isle of the Dead*, repeats the shape of the fire pit, but encircles only cold water. An ice tower guards the opening where a boat drifts aimlessly at the mercy of the elements, carrying three fragile, white-clad figures, the last of whom is not even seen reflected in the water. In the middle of the sky some slender, jagged clouds create an added element of chaos above the great ocean.

Nerdrum continues this same level of visual aggression in *Three Namegivers* (54). The coloring is, if anything, even more unpleasant. The sulphur virtually oozes out of the yellowish-green he has inserted in several places. The harsh play of lines is dominated by diagonals that collide in rather painful intersections, while the bodies of the seated figures are twisted into perpendicular lines running horizontally and vertically. It is strenuous and unpleasant to watch.

The title indicates that it may once again be a meta-picture from Nerdrum's hand – letting his characters comment on something that is happening in the fictitious world he has created for them. In this case someone is naming something previously unnamed in the refuge, an inherently negative activity. The scene might be related to *The Storyteller*, since the man puzzled by the jumper's message now reappears in a one-armed rendering, pointing to his own eye as a sort of law or solution. This is the third time Nerdrum uses the model introduced in *Man against Open Sky*, a painting that in this light also might be a portrait of the interpreter. The almost naive *Mona Lisa* landscape with its identically winding but mirrored roads, may then be the metaphor Nerdrum uses to show that his images are double-coded – on the one hand signifying general, universal entities that are easily recognized, while on the other hand also carrying a more personal and private meaning, which the viewer can only arrive at by some effort. Nerdrum seems to feel that everything at the outset ought to be as wide open and accessible as the sky is to this man, and that the two clouds should be of equal importance, if only he were not so heavily clothed that everything having to do with the body is excluded from the act of perception. Nor does he hear, for his helmet is particularly well padded over the ears, and his hands are so thickly wrapped that his performance is reduced to nothing but shadowboxing. The road, which leads unobstructedly inwards to the left of the stiff, immobile character, is topped at the end by a «one-eyed» mountain; and on the horizon Nerdrum has placed something that can only be seen as a rational, and therefore negative, element in the refuge – the triangular heap of lava. This same mountainous shape has also been placed next to this type of character in the other two paintings, while on «his own» side he has placed a small rock pyramid next to a mountain whose top is identical with the shape of the cap on the young man in the middle of *The Seed Protectors*. The significance of this is so far of less interest than the realization that Nerdrum, if such an interpretation is legitimate, apparently makes use of very private codes in his paintings.

It may be useful to look at a painting such as *Three Namegivers*, since assigning names in a world such as his mental refuge is a very negative undertaking in view of its previous natural state. Such an activity means a not merely

**50.** *Dawn,* 1990. 76 ½ x 112 in.

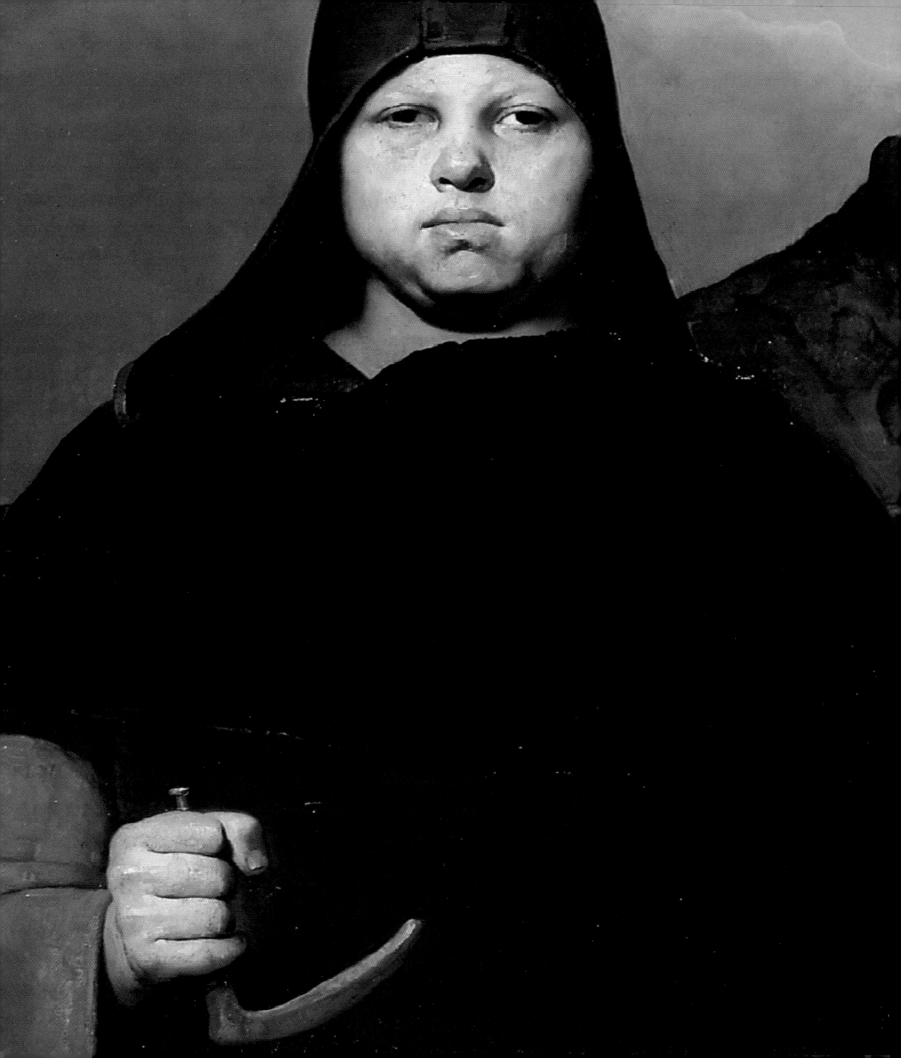

52. *Woman with a Door Handle*, 1990. 45 ¼ x 53 in.

53. *Idiota*, 1990. 68 x 65 ¼ in.

subversive, but also an outright destructive attack on its autonomy and conditions for existence, as this, in Nerdrum's own words, amounts to «restoring misery» and introducing a rational, civilizing factor: «By giving a name to something you kill it. Fix it. Rob it of its power.»[55] However, the notion that a single interpreter, or interpretation, could create unease and chaos in such a universe is not self-evident, especially when Nerdrum as late as in 1987 claimed that this world was completely closed to the spectator. An alien name giver has, however, been given an active role within the borders of this refuge. This may perhaps be understood in light of Nerdrum's comments on the refugee painting – that there may still be villains, but they are no longer being blessed as heroes through the way they are painted. It is thus quite likely that his *Man in Sunset* is a self-portrait showing that he is hurt and that the rational aspect of the triangular cloud was the cause of it. *Woman with a Door Handle*, for which he made the drawing in 1989, is also interesting in this context. My guess is that the darkly clad and shapeless character holds forth what is a totally useless handle to the door Nerdrum sees leading into the refuge, and that this picture can join the lineup of negative reactions to the interpreter's failed attempts at gaining a mental entrance. In *Three Namegivers*, however, there appears to be only one villain. The woman, sitting in the same position as the men in *Dawn*, is wearing the red cloth used in *Wanderer Imitating a Cloud*. Judging by the bandaged head, she is injured. She is also pregnant. The third figure in the painting has fallen face down into the cold water. He is also hurt and can scarcely be counted as a name giver. This must be the wanderer, Nerdrum's nomadic self-image, who displays his scarred back and bares his vulnerable Achilles heel.

At the time he was finishing the painting *Two Men Guiding One Man* (55), Nerdrum gave a rare clue to its interpretation: «*Two Guides* shows how easy it is to overpower the vulnerable, the weak, the pure of heart… One has to choose between good and evil, and what happens in *Two Guides* is that the victim goes along with evil, joins it, as victims often do. Weak individuals are often afraid of embracing freedom . . .»[56] This was as far as Nerdrum was willing to go in his «explanations» at the time, in order to uncover the more personal codes underlying such a universal theme, one has to look elsewhere.

In his collection of aphorisms, *Notater* [Notes], published in 1992, Nerdrum for the first time gave the neutral main key to his use of forms, especially to such landscape shapes as those found in the three mountains behind the figures. The left one is «the aggressive; like the claw of the lion and the agility of the snake.» In the middle is «the amorphous; resting like a leaf, an iceberg.» And lastly there is «the classical; the crystals, the straight forms.»[57] These forms are loaded with significance, but not in any unequivocal pattern. The straight, classical shape he associates with an element of order, but not to a degree that turns it into an antithesis of various elements of chaos. It primarily represents reason and thus the negative in man as well as in civilization. The amorphous form, on the other hand, is nearly always positively loaded and the very archetypal form in nature, while the aggressive one may be positive in reference to Nerdrum's own actions and somewhat negative when associated with those of others, as in, for instance, *Idiota*, where it constitutes an antipode of the crystalline ice tower on the island.

The mountain shapes in *Two Men Guiding One Man* may thus tell us something about who and what these characters might represent. The qualities of the man in the middle are the natural and beautiful ones. He is desirable and therefore worthy of our time and effort. His mountain can even be ascended on a wide spiraling road. The man on the right comes from our miserable world and consequently signifies evil, according to Nerdrum. The one on the left must consequently be Nerdrum himself, who expends all his strength trying to convince the weak and pure at heart to choose good. But he is old. He is also as bearded and toothless as the *Wanderer Imitating a Cloud*, and a bit of the red cloth is attached to his gunsling. This is apparently an important sign; but only two years later did Nerdrum provide a clue to its significance, when an aphorism revealed his use of a color code: «Unhappy love is red. United love is gold. Die in the red – arise in the gold.»[58] It is, of course, possible that the subject of the painting is two men vying to persuade a third, but this interpretation is weakened by Nerdrum's statement. The determined, but somewhat weak, figure in the middle may thus be a woman. The bandaged head recalls the red-clad – and therefore unhappy – woman in *Three Namegivers*, especially since the figure has received a golden belt, which suggests

54. *Three Namegivers,* 1990. 89 x 81 ½ in.

that this person might be not only the desired object, but might also represent united love. Nerdrum had painted the canteen hanging from the belt in exactly the same way once before – in *Portrait of a Girl* (17), which was called *Anine* in its first, 1985, version. It may also be seen lying on the ground in front of the *Woman with Milk*, in which he used the same *Anine* model. The difference is that now there is a small, sharp knife hanging on the outside of the canteen.

The model reappears in *One Storysinger* (56), Nerdrum's second portrayal of a couple after his 1986 *Black Cloud*. Now the woman lies tensely sleeping in a right-angled semi-fetal position. Nerdrum has draped her in the same golden hide as in Sleeping Twins, but a knife has almost unnoticeably found its way into a fold. The sleeping pad has the same red that glows softly in the black, pointed heap of lava. The figure that may be seen to represent Nerdrum is seated, half-blind, lopsided, and amputated atop a blunted rock formation furnished with snakelike varicose veins, howling out his sad song. He is wearing the same white lambskin that once enclosed the pregnant pair of twins, and a fleecy cloud has settled on the amorphous neighboring mountain like a rearing sleeping bag. In the distance a triangular mountain can be seen, and memory is his only muse. Commenting on his work at the time, Nerdrum noted: «I try to bring my images out of the local and into the universal sphere, where man does not possess nature but is an anxious part of it.»[59] Fear and anxiety had now invaded his world. There was trouble in Utopia.

The enemy finally comes forth in the explosively ag-

gressive *Contra Natura* (57), where even the title – Against Nature – indicates that Nerdrum has now felt compelled to leave his recent objective of making a painting at once beautiful and ugly. In this case there is no anatomical beauty, no lovingly painted flesh, and no reposeful natural forms. Everything is consistently hideous and jarringly awful. The crystalline staves of the jagged cliff are formed by Icelandic basalt stone; and, to make things even clearer, the triangular mountain wakes under a murky sky, placed right at the angle where the deformed creature juts out. Such expressive power had earlier been seen in the sculptures of Einar Jonsson;[60] but Nerdrum may also have picked up some visual formulas from Eilif Peterssen's painting *Judas Iscariot*, which both in form and content is related to this grotesque vision (fig.). For the long-necked traitor's black hood has been fastened with a ribbon that forms a Christian cross, which has a golden ring attached. This sign is so distinct that one wonders whether it is not a similar cross being formed by the seated figures in *Three Namegivers*. Instead of a torch, however, Nerdrum's Judas holds a huge knife, threatening the small man in the boat with it. Equipped with only one oar, this figure still represents the forces of light, since he lifts his torch as a counterweight to the evil killer. He is bound to lose this fight, for the time was long passed when nature represented man's salvation in Nerdrum's paintings. Now even the unnatural could win. So what comfort was there in nature´s always winning in the long run? The damage had already been done.

Odd Nerdrum had entered dangerous waters, and now he even disclosed thoughts that indicated a significant change in his personal situation compared to the one that in the early eighties had formed the basis for his flight into the security of nature and the harmony of man in the refuge: «But I do not believe that harmony can be experienced by anyone but unconscious people,» he said, as if to underline the absence of a refuge outside «the blood-filled life,» as he now called reality. And he added: «Creating beauty is the exact opposite of beauty.»[61] His world had come apart, and it was as hideous to live in as to paint. In what had once been a mental refuge a mental inferno was now in progress.

Eilif Peterssen: *Judas Iscariot,* 1887. Lillehammer Kunstmuseum.

55. *Two Men Guiding One Man*, 1990. 72 ¾ x 80 ¾ in.

**56.** *One Storysinger*, 1990.  54 x 68 in.

57. *Contra Natura*, 1990. 59 x 79 in.

# THE SELF-REVEALER

IN THE SPRING OF 1991 FIVE YEARS HAD PAST SINCE Nerdrum last made a self-portrait, *Man with Seeds*. This was very strange for an artist who was so openly preoccupied with having his own life confirmed. But in June 1988, only two months after having read the manuscript of my first book, Nerdrum participated in a television program on narcissism where he read a statement telling about himself:

*As a child I was a lonely person. I had no one to share my thoughts. I was not even accepted among the losers. I was a beggar in the world of the others.*
*The person I saw in the mirror was myself. I reflected myself in my own eyes, not in those of others. Thereby I discovered the gold in my own veins, and I became king in my own kingdom. I became the standard of beauty in my own world, and no longer dependent on the others.*
*I live this hidden life, which has nothing to do with other people, through my self-portraits. I don't show myself to the others, I show myself only to my own mirror image – in a dialogue between me and the image I see. And I arise from the sickbed. I am the lover, the stupid hero, the beautiful one in the sunset. I relish my delicious body. I am the old faithful. In other words: the life of a hero.*
*I am in everyone and reappear in everybody. It takes one to know one . . .*
*I am the shining miracle that no one sees. But once they see me and understand what they are seeing, I will be farthest away.*[1]

Aside from being a hint that one might expect to find Nerdrum represented as a character in paintings not readily identifiable as self-portraits, this was also a clear sign that he so far felt misunderstood or inadequately recognized by his surroundings. To someone who had studied his work both by looking at the paintings and by paying attention to his statements, this was also a problem. There was no immediate reason for distrusting his statements, nor for leaving them out of the interpretation of his work. No doubt the paintings could be both ambiguous and multi-faceted. The personal level, or his own experiences, preferences, and visions, always provided the foundation for the kind of general level to be found in the paintings as mythical and other symbolic references. It did thus not follow from his refusal to state his intentions – as they would be regarded by critics and art historians alike as a dictate in the interpretation of his work – that what he did say in many cases amounted to verbal camouflage and, at worst, an obstacle blocking the understanding of his paintings.

One example of this took place at the end of 1986, shortly after I became acquainted with Nerdrum and interviewed him for the Nordic art magazine *Siksi*. In answer to a direct question about his reasons for using the type of landscape and figures found in his paintings, he made this statement: «My pictures do not relate to society, only to themselves. They are introverted. The landscapes and characters seek no contact with you. You stand outside, looking in at this world as through a keyhole. They do not know of your existence, and they are also indifferent to you because they are living their own lives.»[2] A spectator and interpreter of what could be seen through the keyhole could then not automatically assume that he himself would be included in this world, if he did not discover the unrevealed but intended connections. Nor was it reasonable to conclude that an observer and imaginative presenter of whatever finds were discovered in the available material, would be a «name giver» capable of seriously disturbing this world from within. Given a plausible number of three paintings that include the interpreter among those made in the late eighties – and at least two in which he shows his own reaction to the interpretation – the face value of Nerdrum's statements might seem dubious. Such a realization means that allowances have to be made concerning the veracity of some of his utterances, at least in terms of conventional expectations. It is also clear that other statements had become more precise because he felt unrecognized in his own work, as his declaration shows. Finally the assumption is strengthened that his imagery is highly autobiographical, and that anything related to his own life may appear in coded form in his paintings. As one might have suspected ever since *Amputation* and *The Murder of Andreas Baader*, it comes as no surprise that Nerdrum was capable of wielding his brush the way Caravaggio did his sword.

The great upheaval taking place in Nerdrum's life at this time, as well as his great need to express it in his paintings, eventually also found its way into his statements. In a speech made at the student union in Bergen in September 1991 Nerdrum apparently decided to lift the veil and give a clearer indication of the kind of world depicted in his pictures and the means used:

*If you fall asleep by the wheel of a car, death will occur against the nearest rock. If you fall asleep on horseback, the horse will stop by the rock. When the rider got the idea that the horse was inferior to him, man began losing touch with his subconscious. Wordlessly the subconscious lets you know long before consciousness, by which time it is often too late. By then it has already happened. The self-deceived heart is the rider who has whipped his horse to death.*
*Our real choices always belong to the subconscious. They are sensual and always in search of the best . . . Our choices give us away; we choose ourselves in what we prefer . . .*
*Self-revelation is enriching. An artist who does not reveal himself is soon unmasked by the viewer. If a work of art is not personal and naked, the viewer will lose interest or consider it superficial. We have to understand that only a few are to reveal themselves to us, and that not everyone should reveal themselves to one another. If that happens, everyone will hide in a semi-revelation, in which all that is great is abused in a wider context.*
*The individualist, or self-revealer, is metaphorical and a user of intrigue. The whole world may get to know his innards. His life is being exposed. The clad – those who belong to the scene – feel strong in their collective garb. They regard the self-revealer as stupid. The look of greatest sincerity in Rembrandt's eyes is seen by them as submissiveness . . . The strictly personal turns universal by its convincing self-revelation . . .*
*Modern art cannot be exempt from history. It will fail by its lack of sensual presence. Modern art lacks flesh. We use our skin for seeing as much as we use our thoughts. We prefer anything that reminds us of our body, however unwittingly. Why do lamps made of white opaque glass intrigue us so? Because it*

*reminds us of mother's milk. Rembrandt reminds us of our abdomen, where all is warm, soft, and dark. The sky in Turner's paintings reminds us of the blue color of our veins. Others paint skies that look like skies, but to us Turner's sky has a sensual touch of ourselves . . .*
*Intimately rendered substance is all I believe in. By living substance I mean something that cannot be divided. It has a core. The flesh closes lovingly around the core. Only when the idea of substance has been gratified in the sensually painted can we get into a story . . .*
*When choosing art from the past we become treacherously sensual . . . When it comes to our own age, we straighten our backs, strangely fettered in our choices . . . We become slaves to the European clock . . .*
*Substance is the timeless reality . . . Rembrandt was most faithful to substance. We always seek back to the art that carries a notion of substance, of nakedness. Rembrandt might be seen as private in a sense. This means that he comes close to our skin, close to our body. Substance does not consider ideals or a linear view of history. Substance simply exists within itself, amorphously resting, just like the subconscious . . .*
*Substance, the subconscious, and sensuality are related concepts. In trying to reach out to one another we look to the most basic in each other. At heart we are simple. On the surface we are often deeply complex, trying to deceive one another with tales about our souls, as metaphysics covers the real reason like a layer of glaze. In the inner life of our minds we are embarrassingly concrete. The reason for longing is never abstract. There is always a specific reason for a problem of the mind . . . The subconscious is not abstract. It corresponds precisely and strongly to substance and reality. Hence it requires knowledge to depict and recreate it. For our inner life longs to be explained. The sublime, that which moves our hearts, is a direct and concrete attempt to reach the secretive ego. The convincing work of art is the rider in harmony with his horse . . .*
*We will never ever be able to create life. But life can shine through us in a work of art. We can all become timeless if we dare.[3]*

Of course, Odd Nerdrum is here speaking of himself, and there is every reason to believe that our understanding of his imagery will be enriched if we believe him at his word: on the one hand that he is an unreserved self-revealer in his work, on the other, that there is a specific and concrete reason for the problems and the conflicts he depicts from his life. Above all, that both in life and art, in words as well as actions, «metaphysics» is merely a surface of glazes covering the actual reason and the real significance. If this is true at the level of intention, it puts all of the previous so-called metaphysical interpretations of what Nerdrum may have meant in his paintings into a class of subjective fantasy, including the interpretations of this writer. It is, of course, possible to interpret his work as an expression of totally different socio-psychological conditions than the ones he himself is aware of, or to regard both the painter and his work as media for more wide-ranging processes in society at large. However, when trying to understand what Nerdrum himself may have wanted to put into his images, his own life is the most important source. The most dramatic conclusion to be drawn from these observations is that his paintings – at least after the mid-eighties – have also not been double-coded. There is no longer any support for the claim that Nerdrum has consciously coded his images, for them to be decoded by the aid of a dictionary of symbols, thereby forming stories other than the intended, strictly personal ones. His paintings carry basically only one code, his highly private one, even if some of the symbols and archetypal forms used may also have a universal meaning. As pointed out by himself, it is only through complete and fully convincing self-revelation that the strictly personal can become universal.[4] In this he introduces still another problem of interpretation, since it is difficult to arrive at a more precise understanding of his highly private codes by merely looking at the pictures and reading his words on paper. It demands a fairly privileged interpreter, a participating observer with access to certain kinds of private information, not to the key to the code itself, but a knowledge of important events in Nerdrum's life and of his «seismographic» responses to them. As he never gets more specific than to strongly suggest that the paintings deal with himself and his exposed innards – presumably true also of his earlier production – while he at the same time gives verbal warnings against the complexity of his own use of signs, there is still ample room for getting lost and presenting interpretations that do not reflect the issue at hand. It is a risk worth taking, even though a failure may lead to an inglorious position within his paintings.

Just before Nerdrum stood forth in his Bergen speech

to expose himself as a consistent «self-revealer» in his work, there had been dramatic changes in his personal life. Since 1984 he had had a close and very special relationship with one of his young pupils. In the portrait he painted of her in 1985 she was called Anine, and subsequently she appeared in his paintings on a number of occasions both as a model and as a metaphorical figure. There may have been any number of reasons for his fascination with this girl, but undoubtedly one of the most important ones was that he recognized himself in her. When he repeated the motif in *Portrait of a Girl* ten years later, using another model, he gave the character his own features. Nerdrum has said that «the melancholic gaze is security,» so he must also have recognized Munch's *Sick Child* and the faces of Botticelli's women in his pupil, perhaps even his own mother, whom she resembled.[5] Their relationship was very intense, and for long periods she lived in his studio. They were often seen together in the city or out travelling. This was problematic for his previous companion, with whom he had three daughters, one of them recently born. It was also a problem for the girl, who did not want to «share» him with anyone. Eventually it also became a problem for Nerdrum, when his surroundings objected to his double life. He had to make a choice, but made none.

In the fall of 1989 his beloved pupil was admitted to the National Academy of Art in Oslo. That same year students and staff alike had openly acknowledged their hatred of Nerdrum by interrupting a lecture given by the Swedish art historian Madeleine von Heland when she referred to Odd Nerdrum as an important artist within international figurative painting. Led by a teacher they chanted abusive taunts against the absent Nerdrum.[6] With some justification he now began worrying about losing his beloved, and soon she found a new companion among her fellow students. He may be the one to turn up as a rival in *Two Men Guiding One Man*, which was completed in 1990, and probably also in *Contra Natura*, where he becomes a threat, using the destructive symbol Nerdrum now called «The Loveknife.»[7] This instrument also appears in duplicate in *Twins with Knives* (58), in which the new couple has formed a lethal Siamese alliance. But in *Man Bitten by a Snake* (59), for which he made the drawing in early 1991, all three are metaphorically present. This is where evil enters Nerdrum's naked and vulnerable world in the form of a poisonous snake that bites him in the leg. The hairless body twists in convulsions, and his face is deformed by pain. The synchronously striding couple continue their carefree chat, using an elated «George-Bush gesture,» leaving their victim behind in the darkened landscape. The man wearing the jaunty gold cap points to the snake-bitten loser, forming a cross with his fingers – a symbol that Nerdrum pinned to both the girl and his rival and regarded as the antithesis of the moral law of nature prevailing in his realm. But no law whatsoever could help him when what he had long feared actually happened.

In the spring of 1991 the girl left Nerdrum, which sent him into a long and severe crisis. Judging by *Idiota*, the relationship with the woman he had lived with for years had come to an end, and he had finally made up his mind to choose his *Anine*. He was so sure of the durability of their relationship, despite her life at the Academy, where the atmosphere was militantly hostile to Nerdrum. He was mistaken. For several months he waited, hoping that she would return, until he himself grabbed a knife, went to her home, and slashed all the portrait-drawings he had given her. The way he described it in *Sleeping Couple* (60), which was originally titled *Dying Couple*, their love had now gone, and, with it, a considerable part of themselves. He had brought home black lava sand from Iceland and now mixed it into the paint virtually as a sign of mourning. Wrapped in black hides, the shapes of their bodies echo the distant mountain bathed in a golden glow. Soon the light will fade and only the triangle will be left. In the grayish-brown, dissolved *Self-Portrait with Closed Eyes* (61), he finally steps forward to reveal his inner darkness, a theme which he time and again touched on in his self-revealing aphorisms: «So rejected that nothing can sustain me – except anxiety.»[8] There were also other emotions: «Bitterness dictates, and I work like mad,» or the experience of «The evil that I know so well, since I am myself evil.»[9] The rival soon disappeared from his imagery, but his years with Anine, and the conflict that ended that relationship, had left deep marks on his soul.

In the spring of 1992 Nerdrum wrote the introduction in the catalogue for an exhibition of a Rembrandt painting that was organized by this writer at Bergen Art Museum. In it he spoke of how Rembrandt, in an alchemist spirit, often painted golden objects into his paintings, and then concluded: «It is a reminder of man stepping out of the darkness, just like the gold to be released from the dark leaden walls. The gold of the human mind is the timeless gaze that belongs to eternity.»[10] He called his contribution «Twin Souls,» a verbal reference to the similarities in Titian and Rembrandt, as found in their later works; but Nerdrum may have thought as much of his beloved. For «Twin Souls» was also the title of the first comprehensive show of his paintings dealing with the problems of love, exhibited that fall at the Museum of Contemporary Art in Oslo.[11] He now openly declared that «luck, unhappiness, and conflicts in love are themes that recur in my paintings.»[12] On another occasion he elaborated: «I have only depicted my own life. My technique is a language I myself understand and use . . . Hamsun has written the most beautiful love letter in the world in *Victoria* – and used his language for that. I use mine . . .»[13] *Blind Wanderer* (62) may probably be considered such a letter of love. Here a one-legged nomad has fumbled along in his inner darkness and has come across the two gowned twin souls on the ground. Nerdrum wrote: «The reunion in the recollection results in twins – close to one another.»[14] The blind cataleptic is dressed in red, searching for love, and unhappy. The couple is united in gold, and the girl is once again shown as pregnant. She is holding a twig with a single leaf. His is bare: «A twig,» explained Nerdrum, while the painting was still a sketch, «was the symbol of manly virility… .»[15] Taken literally, this meant a pretty sad state of affairs. The same might be said of the characters in the three nocturnal portraits he painted later that year. *Boy with Twig* (63) has only one leaf left on his, while the *Man with Shield and Stone* (64) displays what is left of his love in his crippled hand. And the severely burnt *Man with Torch* (65) barely manages to step forth from the leaden wall carrying his faint life-light, or «the heavy, dark wave,» as he also called his mood.[16] When Nerdrum's burn-injured model committed suicide shortly after the completion of the picture, one can only imagine the impact it had on him.

The hope of being reunited with his love may also have been the theme in *Five Persons around a Water Hole* (66), drawn a few months before her final departure. The figures in the foreground are at least carrying the attributes of both, despite their excess of fat. The young character on the left is a symbolic portrait of himself as a young man –

58. *Twins with Knives,* 1991. 43 ¼ x 46 in.

60. *Sleeping Couple*, 1991. 43 ¼ x 39 ½ in.

**59.** *Man Bitten by a Snake*, 1992. 93 x 105 ¼ in.

**62.** *Blind Wanderer*, 1992. 94 ¾ x 108 ¾ in.

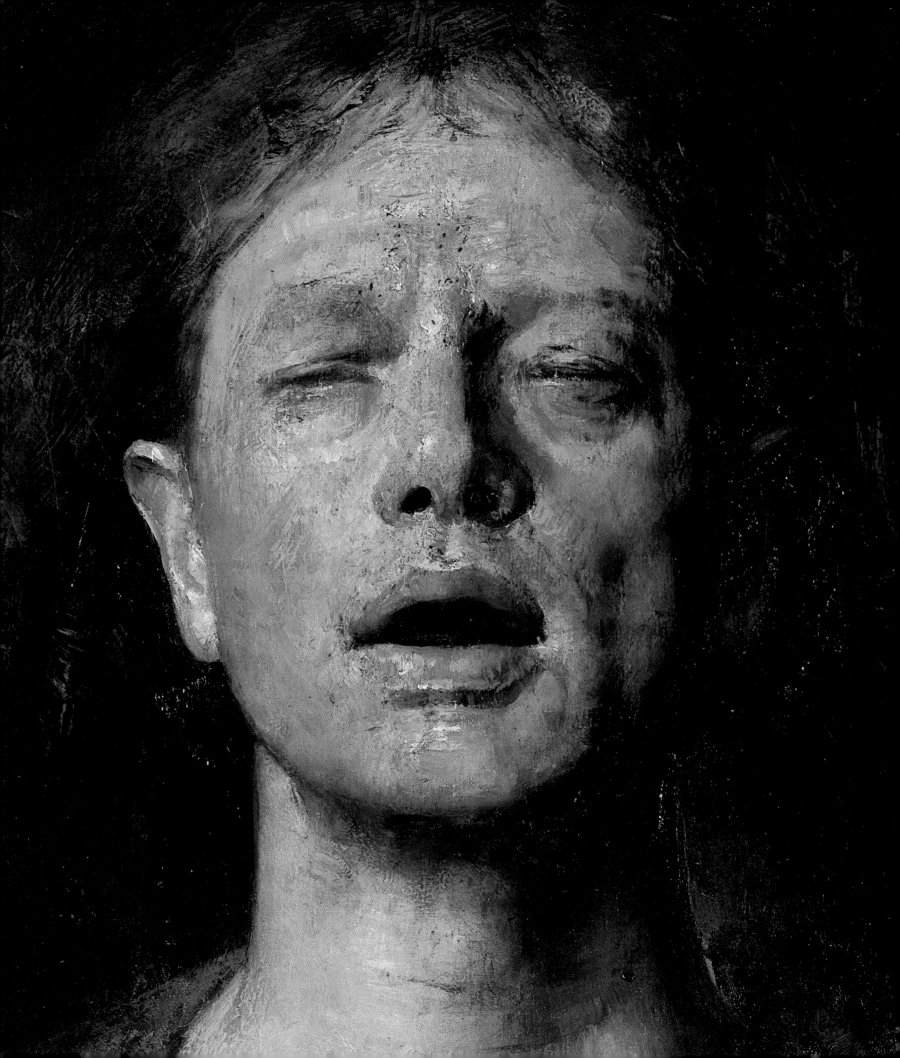

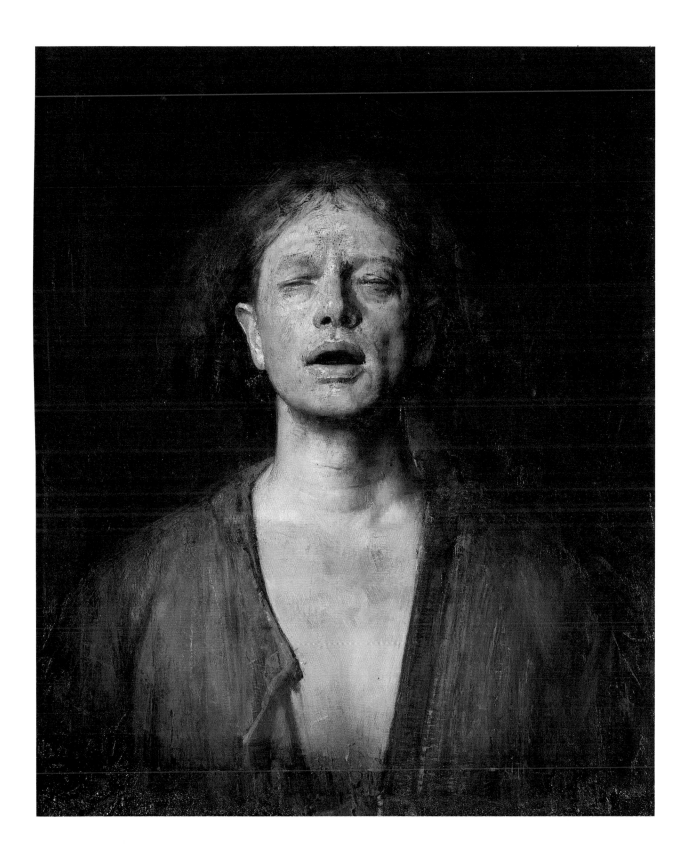

**61.** *Self-Portrait with Closed Eyes,* 1991. 27 ½ x 31 ½ in.

**64.** *Man with Shield and Stone,* 1992. 53 x 39 ½ in.

**63.** *Boy with Twig,* 1992. 35 ½ x 29 ½ in.

**65.** *Man with Torch*, 1992. 35 ½ x 29 ½ in.

**66.** *Five Persons around a Water Hole,* 1992. 111 x 139 ¾ in.

his daughter Nora serving as his model – and placed in the middle is the male, respectively the female, principle of ideal pairing, as if before a wedding of two related basic values. All the figures have been painted with only one leg showing, and they all gaze wistfully down into the golden water. Nerdrum's notion of dying in the red and arising in the gold is probably also behind his bathing *Hermaphrodite* (67), in which the entire landscape appears transformed by the dispersing banks of fog. In this dry and roughly painted picture, which took him four years to finish, he has used some of the symbolism of alchemy, in the form of an androgynous synthesis, to express his longing for reconciliation. For when the sulphur, represented by both the bank of earth and the voyeur, is combined with the pale quicksilver in the hermaphrodite's hair, gold is created through the alchemist metamorphosis. Thus the picture reflects – by its style as well as its form and symbolism – Nerdrum's methodological kinship with the alchemist's formula *solve et coagula* – dissolve and merge. The same may also be true of *A Father Finding His Son* (1), and then in a double sense, because here it actually looks as if he has combined two different longings for reunification in a single image. The most obvious is the father, who has an injured left arm and some love-seeking red close to his body, finding his son on a golden hide. But it may at the same time reflect Nerdrum's longing for his female twin soul, as he is lying there, contorted by pain next to the knife and the canteen. The reunion of the souls has been accomplished in the boat passing the twin mountains, but the triangular mountain looms on the horizon.

The last of the three motifs that Nerdrum drew in early 1991, and painted a year later, was *The Red Cape* (68). The date may be important for the understanding of the coding of the picture, since it was conceived before his final break with Anine. There is an almost Poussin-like atmosphere in the warm hues of the archaic landscape. The figures are running along a bloodred earth, which passes into the black lake with no perspectival intermediary. On the left stands a broken rock column in front of an amorphous mountain, while the right-hand mountain has a more aggressive form. In the center a red triangular mountain is outlined against the horizon, straight above the rather civilized human dwelling. It was the first time since *Man with Seeds* that Nerdrum used his own features in a

painting, but he himself would scarcely want to expose the old man, in the way a son drains knowledge from his father. Since he often sees himself in others, and especially in *Anine*, it may be she pointing to herself while tearing the cape in a dethroning gesture from Nerdrum's own alterego – the old one-eyed man with a beard. For this cape is more mauve than red, making this drama signify something more than stolen love alone. Although it is possible to see the little man with the spear as engaged in demolishing their home by his metaphorical act, he may also be piercing something in the cavity of the womb. Our current knowledge of Nerdrum's codes makes this kind of reading possible, especially when relating this scene to the drama taking place in his imagery beginning in early 1986. Starting with *Man with Seeds*, continuing through the pregnant *Anine* characters in single and double versions, to the black clouds of death and the lifeless, doubled face in *Sole Morte*, something definitely seems to have been conceived, only to be quickly lost again.

This suspicion is strengthened by *Man with Catfish* (69), in which Nerdrum appears as a lone wanderer under a sulphurous, nocturnal sky. The heavy man sits in a monopedic pose by the abyss, wiggling his toes like a baby and wearing the white bonnet of innocence on his head. In the depths between a couple of Scylla and Charybdis cliffs he has fished out his ugly catch and is cradling it gently in his lap. His knife hangs on his staff, leaving us to wonder if it signifies the reason for the tragedy, or if it is the tool soon to be used in slaying his disgusting creature, as he is finally able to rid himself of the remains of the inverted symbol of fertility. This symbol reappears equally brutal and cruel a couple of years later in *Woman with Fish* (70). Here both the man and the woman carry spears, and both look at the suffering monster of a fish with equal terror. The man is bald and one leg has been amputated. One eye is askew. On the beach lie the remains of a rectangular box, and a bit farther away a haloed shipwreck with a strip of red cloth attached to the mast. Nerdrum could hardly have told his self-revealing story in plainer terms. Were it not for that poor fish they had once speared, their relationship would still be intact. The lovers are seen embracing for their ride into the sunset in the background. But behind them is the irretrievably broken column, and the triangular mountain looms on this horizon.

67. *Hermaphrodite*, 1992 – 1996. 80 ¾ x 83 in.

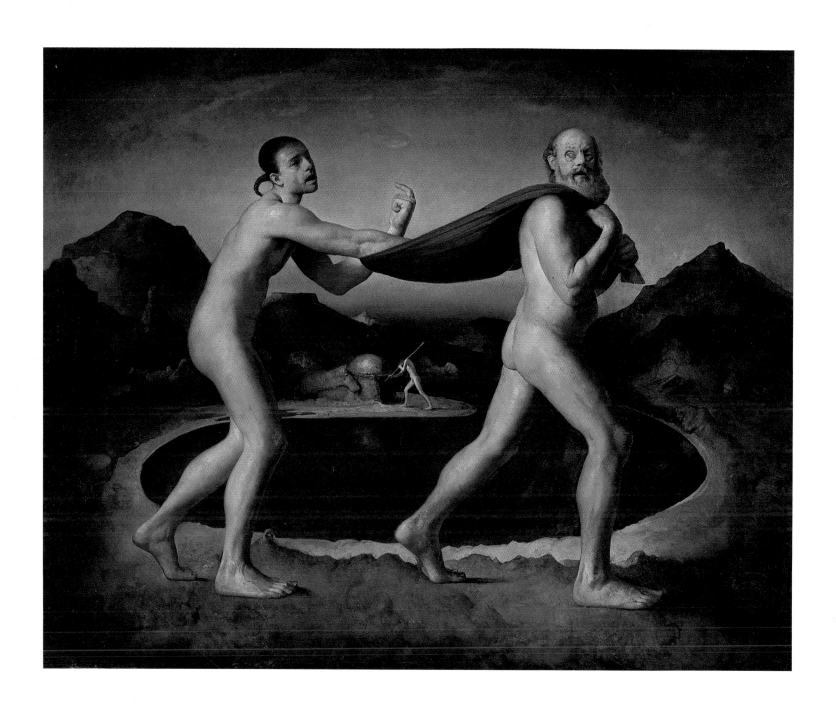

**68.** *The Red Cape,* 1992. 59 ½ x 73 ¼ in.

**69.** *Man with Catfish,* 1992. 72 ¼ x 82 ¼ in.

70. *Woman with Fish*, 1994. 65 x 61 in.

In the scratched, ashen *Self-Portrait with Eyes Half Closed* (71), which Nerdrum began working on in 1991, he is barely able to see himself. Dense darkness still ruled his world, and the grief might as well be expressed in the melancholy look of death in the eyes of an animal's decapitated head, as it is in *Man with a Horse's Head* (72). Here it becomes clear what he had meant in his Bergen speech, when he had spoken of the horse whipped to death. He was speaking of himself, now showing that the deed had been done by the same person who held the «Loveknife.» This use of visual metaphors is repeated in the sand-black and overwhelmingly gloomy *Dying Couple* (73), where Gericault's painting of the decapitated heads, which Nerdrum had seen so many times in Stockholm, gained new relevance (fig.). Here the faithless rider had «whipped» his horse to death using the same knife once again. The wanderer lies dying, his body contorted in sexual convulsions, while the woman's corresponding spasms are caused by the «self-deceived heart,» which has stopped beating by itself. But the closest Nerdrum has ever come to his goal of making the strictly personal universal through convincing self-revelation is in his violent drama *Woman Killing Injured Man* (74). Once again we recognize the nocturnal scenario from Guido Reni's painting, but Nerdrum has instead let his small background figures put out their torches of love in the cold water of the great ocean. There is no doubt that this is also a run for life. Her torch lies long snuffed out on the ground, while his still smolders. Soon it will also be extinguished, the same way his terrified equine eyes are about to burst from the bleeding wound that has been so cruelly inflicted on his head. In conversation Nerdrum has admitted that he barely survived this stabbing. One begins to realize what parts

of his psyche have provided the source of all that sensual richness and visual power embedded in their bodies. And a closer look makes it clear that this picture is at least as convincing in its flesh-painting as in terms of self-revelation.

Nerdrum's life was not merely bleak and gloomy. In the early nineties he had found the peace of mind needed to paint a couple of new objects (75,76), and in 1992 he met his wife-to-be, Turid Spildo (77). She was a folk musician and came from a rural area on the west coast of Norway. To Nerdrum she represented a ray of light in the darkness, as shown in a small study for a self-portrait that same year, where he is actually looking at himself again (78). They have two sons – Bork, born in 1993, and Øde, born in 1995 – and each time Nerdrum painted them shown horizontally, as *The Baby* (14). Bork was also portrayed vertically as *Newborn* (79). It is hard to say whether or not it is evident that he had his first son the same year that he found his father. But on the left at the bottom of the painting there is a sharp claw coming out from the hide where the baby is resting, and next to it there is something resembling a sheet of paper. He has also placed a small golden bonnet beneath the baby's drawn-up bundling, similar to the one that appears a year later in *Girl with Butterfly* (80), so that the same bonnet that accompanied the birth of his son is placed on the girl whose life is transformed into a passing memory.

Despite his new-found happiness the trauma was apparently not behind him. In *Man with a Woman's Head* (81) he returns to the grave, and to «the memory that can never be grasped – that can never become raw flesh again.»[17] Dressed in a small, golden piece of leather, he has dug up her severed head, using the same spade he once used when sowing his unlucky thirteen seeds. The sharp knife is there, but so is the snake and the silky, soft cotton grass. There is an ambivalence in his caressing of the dead girl's head, for attached to the dark hood covering his beaten and bandaged head there is a tiny plume of victory. Since Nerdrum has also given one of these to the ambiguously attired, one-eyed *Dr. Kagul* (82), who has a red belt across his golden vest, it can be read as a hint of recovery. Only a hint, though, for in *Sigmund* (83) he is once again back in the red color-code of unhappy love, this time wearing a leather band similar to the one that

Théodore Gericault: *The Decapitated Heads,* Nationalmuseum, Stockholm.

**71.** *Self-Portrait with Eyes Half-Closed,* 1991–1993. 43 ¼ x 39 ½ in.

**72.** *Man with a Horse's Head,* 1993. 58 ½ x 61 ½ in.

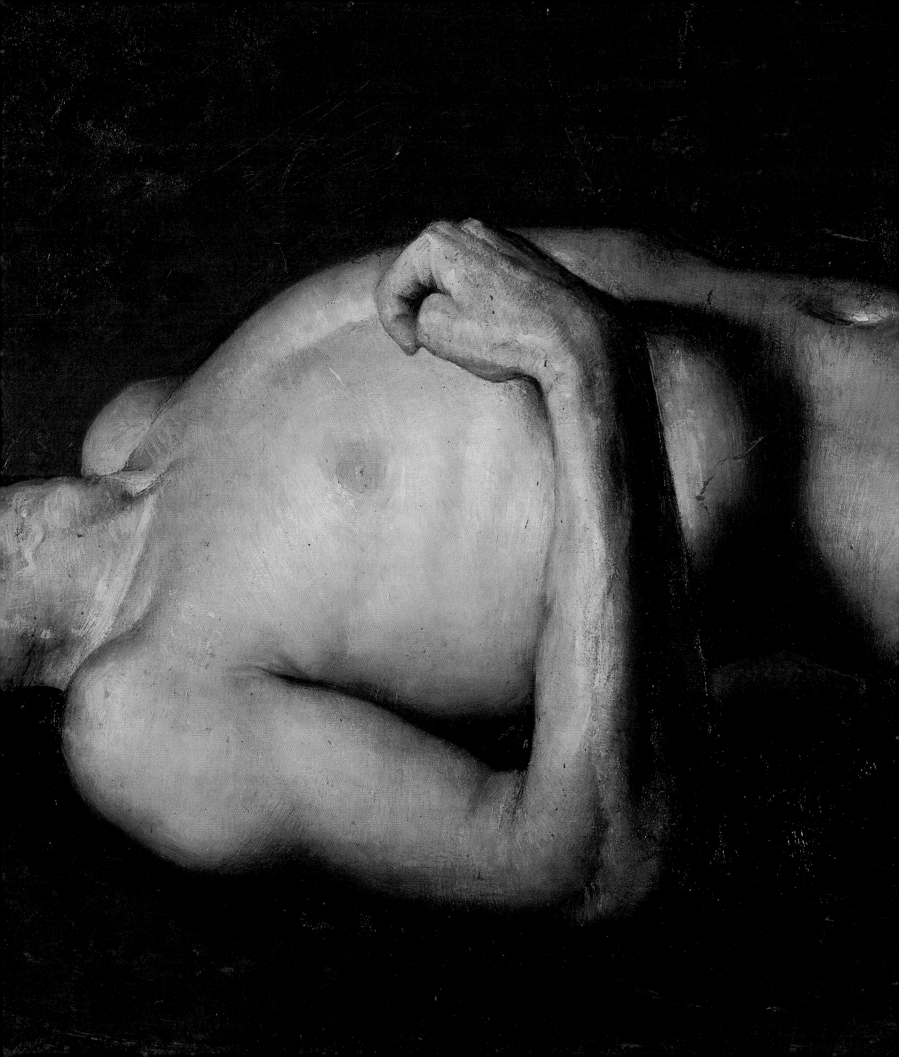

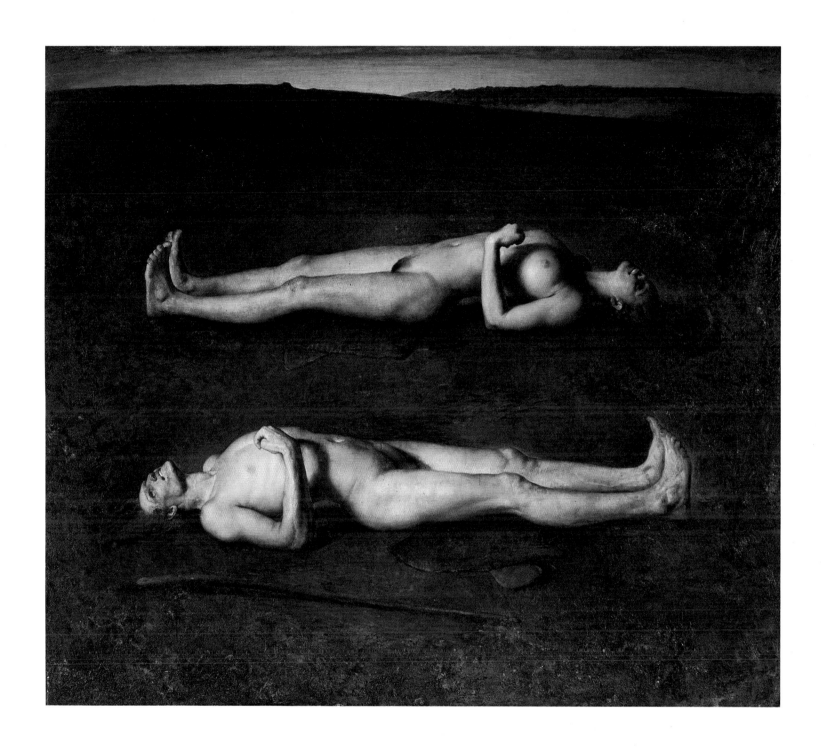

73. *Dying Couple*, 1993. 96 ¾ x 107 ¾ in.

74. *Woman Killing Injured Man,* 1994. 78 ¾ x 114 ¼ in.

75. *A Pear*, 1990. 14 ½ x 17 in.

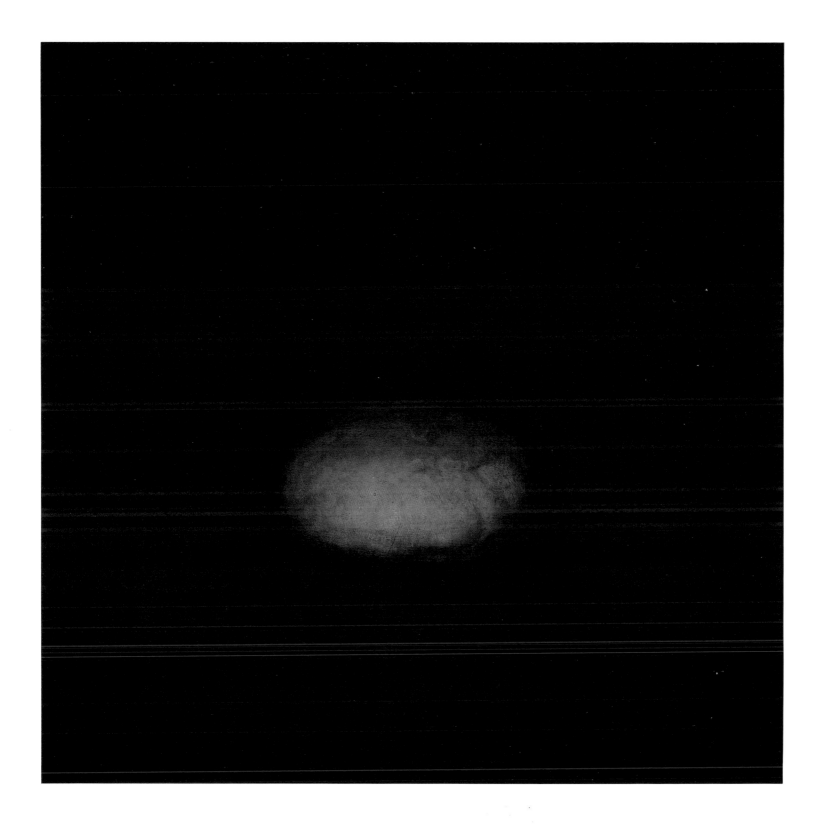

76. *Bread,* 1991. 27 ½ x 25 ½ in.

78. *Self-Portrait at Ystaas,* 1992. 17 ¾ x 13 ¾ in.

77. *Turid*, 1992. 17 ¾ x 13 ¾ in.

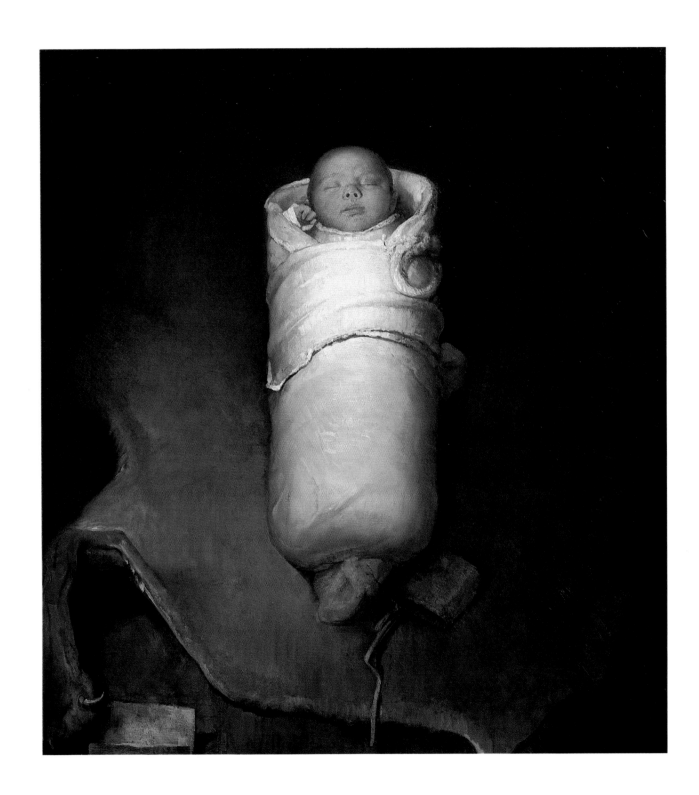

**79.** *Newborn,* 1993. 27 ½ x 30 ¼ in.

80. *Girl with Butterfly*, 1994. 72 ¾ x 17 ¾ in.

**81.** *Man with a Woman's Head,* 1994. 72 ¾ x 57 in.

82. *Dr. Kagul*, 1994. 35 ½ x 31 ½ in.

**83.** *Sigmund,* 1994. 31 ½ x 27 ½ in.

encircled the head in the *Anine* portrait nine years earlier.

A new book about Nerdrum's paintings was published in the fall of 1994. The book was written by his friend, a professor in the history of ideas, Jan-Erik Ebbestad Hansen, who had followed Nerdrum for nearly thirty years, and who had been working on a biography of him since 1987. In 1992 he had assisted Nerdrum in the editing of his book of aphorisms, *Notater*, and he had also written the introduction to the book, the most lucid collection of statements and personal confidences Nerdrum had ever produced. The publication of Ebbestad Hansen's book was eagerly awaited, not only due to developments in Nerdrum's work since 1988, but also because he had been a very vocal critic of my previous book, an interpretative attempt which he felt suffered from «an incompetent use of images and concepts.»[18] He chose to give his view of Nerdrum's work without including a single cryptic declaration or self-interpretation that might reflect Nerdrum's own temperament and views. Instead he placed Nerdrum in a context where his artistic development and position were seen to reflect the general ideological trends of the previous thirty years. Nerdrum's own view and self-assessment – which is in fact the thinking that will eventually materialize in his art – is that he has always chosen a course of his own, clearly emphasized in aphoristic declarations such as: «The follower never comes first,» and «Where I walk there are no roads, but the others follow and put up road signs.»[19] Perhaps the most surprising aspect of the book, however, was that it left the impression that Nerdrum's work was still limited to a critique of our civilization, expressed through a succession of archetypal themes and traditional myths. Although the author made interesting observations on the parallels to the alchemist's symbolic universe, his treatise left totally untouched the artistic mind that sought its self-confirmation through those codified images. Nowhere in his book did he mention the dramatic events in Nerdrum's life that virtually jumped out of the paintings, nor did he devote a single phrase to identify Nerdrum as a clearly autobiographical painter commenting on actual situations in his own life. On the background of Nerdrum's visual response to my book, it is not inconceivable that he may have reacted to Ebbestad Hansen's, as well.

If he ever did, the response must be found in *Five Namegivers* (84). The trouble with such an interpretation is that the motif appeared in a sketch as early as 1987, as part of Nerdrum's interest in a rhythmic pentagonal composition and was further developed a couple of years later, after he had seen the mountains at Snæfellnes in Iceland. Considering his general problem with rational name givers at this time, it is still possible to see a connection between the painting and the book. As was true of *Three Namegivers*, one cannot take for granted that the number of potential perpetrators suggested by the title coincides with the role of the figures in the painting. One has to resort to guesswork in an attempt to identify the name givers (if there are any), the victim, and any extras. There is a good chance that the number of figures is determined by compositional needs, with compositional requirements overriding the content. This might explain the introduction of the two figures in the background and their part in creating symmetry and space. The main characters seem to be the three in the foreground, two of them naked and seated in nearly identical positions, while the one on the right turns his back on the others. Close by this figure lies Nerdrum's own attribute – the staff. The extinguished lantern may also refer to him. Only the knife is new in his case, but it is sheathed, perhaps indicating that he has become less dangerous. Above this figure rises an amorphously resting dome-shaped mountain, while the middle figure is sitting below a rational triangular mountain with a lower ridge in the foreground, crowned by a tiny peak. The man on the left has a dark cloud above his head and next to it a more aggressive mountain with a small peak. This peak is repeated in the mountains to the far right, as is the terracing and the bridge across the narrow gorge, where the one on the left has turned into a tiny suspension bridge, while the other is straight and solid. The only similarity between these two figures is that the reddish brown color of the cloth hanging across the leg of the left one is repeated in the wanderer's own cloth. Aside from this, the young man's only distinction is a rather feminine red ribbon around his head, ornamented with rosettes. The slightly older person in the middle has been given a golden animal hide, whose paw has the claws of a predator. He looks at the spectator and points to the hand he holds in front of his mouth. The two figures in the back-

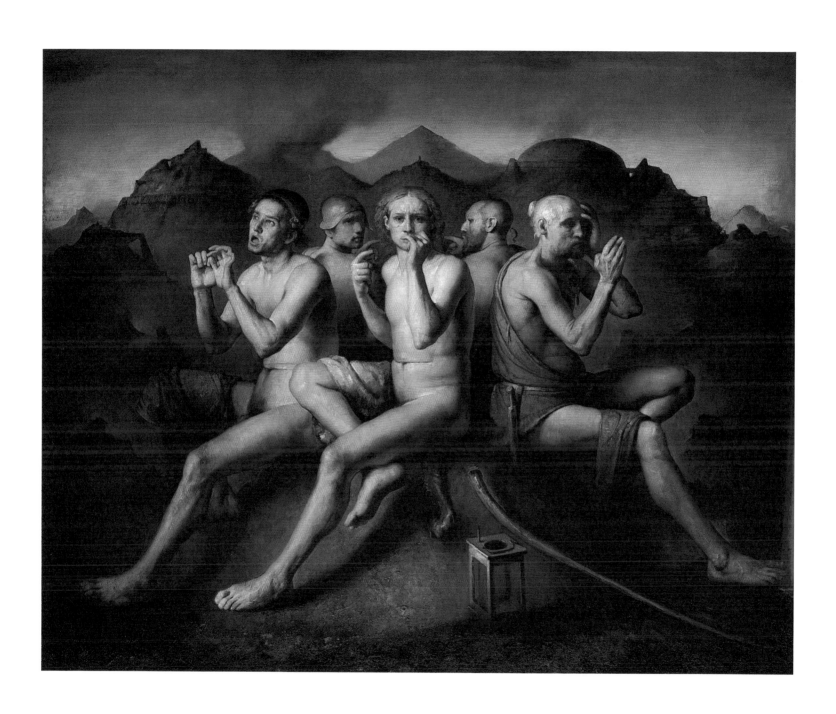

84. *Five Namegivers*, 1994. 74 ¾ x 65 in.

ground are also pointing at him, confirming his central role. These may both be associated with Nerdrum, since the younger one wears the headgear of the character in *Man with a Woman's Head*, and the mature one seems to be the model used in *Wanderer Imitating a Cloud*. The old-timer holds his head in a gesture resembling the one Nerdrum's «artist father figure,» Joseph Grimeland, has a habit of making when seeing or hearing something terrible.[20] The other hand points into the air with the thumb turned inward. The awkward name giver on the left looks longingly for the light coming from the same general direction, fumbling, with an open mouth and a limp tongue. It is hard to be any more specific about this picture, other than noting that if the two naked figures are to be the name givers, it is a big step forward for this type of character compared to the former, heavily clad one.

Nerdrum is, in fact, not in the habit of depicting the fate of others in his work, unless they have a direct bearing on his own. Thus the *Five Namegivers* may as well be interpreted as a portrayal of himself in three different positions and situations, in a sort of «answer» to the naming being done to his work. On the left is the groping and searching one, finding his way in the subconscious; in the middle the knowing, but reticent and silent lion; and, on the right, the one who through painful experiences has become wise or maybe even resigned. For it is quite clear that he was rather concerned about the reception of his paintings. In an aphorism he had written: «The unspeakable – the interpreter made redundant.»[21] There is also a chance that the conflicts between his two interpreters on the one hand, and himself on the other, may have entered his painted world in early 1990, when Ebbestad Hansen published his first review.[22] *Two men Guiding One Man* may initially have dealt with this theme, if the reading suggested by himself at the time was merely camouflage or had entered in a later change of codification as a result of problems in his love life while he was finishing it. In that case Nerdrum himself is the injured victim in the center, while a couple of cheeky and pushy name givers – the older a bit more aggressive than the younger one – try to get him onto their respective side. Determined to hold his ground, he indicates that neither of them has managed to scale his «mountain.» At any rate, these two interpretations do not necessarily exclude one another; but when a

choice has to be made, it is helpful to remember that Nerdrum is a very conscious user of intrigue as a self-revealer in his visual metaphors and that it is his own outlook and self-image that gets projected onto the persons and situations depicted.

Nerdrum must also have had Joseph Grimeland in mind when he painted the figure to the right in *Three Men at Dawn* (85) a year later. The painting is related to *Five Namegivers*, but less complicated in its codes. Three elderly men of roughly the same vintage are seated in a boat on dry land. Their lives are nearly, or completely, over, and in the background three relatively «rational» mountains loom with their rounded-off tops. Nerdrum appears to have painted his three «fathers.» In the bow sits David Sandved, his eyes longingly fixed on the light and the memories, or, as Nerdrum had observed in one of his aphorisms: «Finally old enough for the child to look out from the face.»[23] On the left in the middle ground Nerdrum has placed some clearly architectural shapes of basalt and a large, black hole leading into the ground. On the right sits the introverted Grimeland, who safeguards his secrets in the death grip from the *Dying Couple*, and in the middle is a figure who must be the legal father, Johan Nerdrum – the only dead person in the group. He has turned his head, looking at a sharp boat hook, a shape repeated in the center mountain. Perhaps this is what Nerdrum referred to when he wrote: «Hatred is hereditary. It is unbearable.»[24]

Shortly after Nerdrum completed a series of studies of the pained expression of a dying girl (86–90), his own son, Øde, suddenly fell seriously ill. Doctors who came to the house saw no cause for alarm, but the boy got increasingly worse. In the nick of time Nerdrum himself decided to bring him into the hospital, which probably saved his life. *Baby in Deserted Landscape* (91) shows that the incident left its marks. The baby lies naked and vulnerable on the sulphurous volcanic slope. The cocoon-like swaddling cloth has been slashed open, exposing a swollen belly. A lizard warns of danger and death, but also signifies hope and resurrection. In *The Lifesaver* (92), which was also inspired by the incident with his son, the codes are different. In this version an armed, red-clad «skinhead» has found the abandoned baby in the dark of night. His expression is inscrutable as he holds the child's fate in his large hands

85. *Three Men at Dawn*, 1996. 73 ¾ x 61 in.

 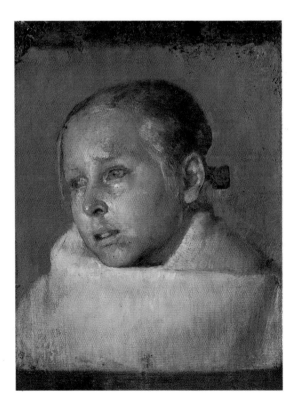

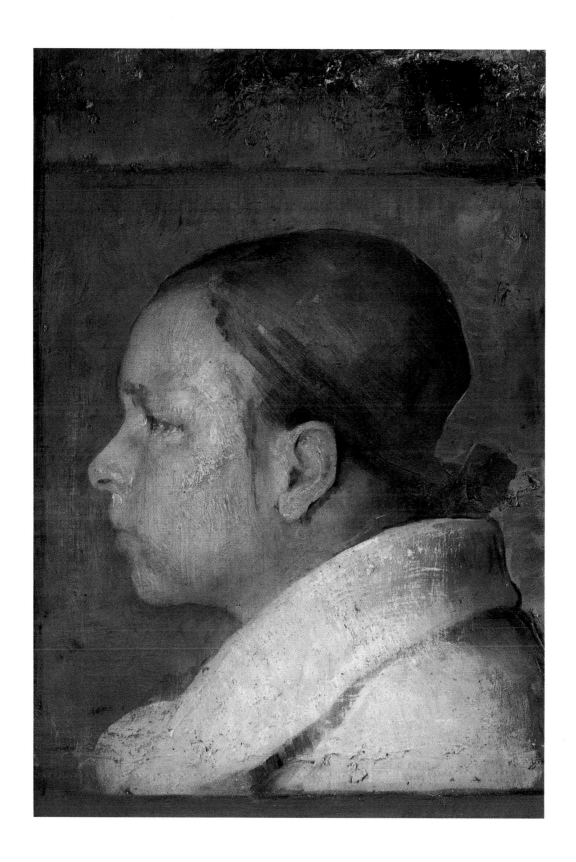

**86-90.** *Studies of Anne Sofie,* 1994 – 95. 15 ¾ x 13 ¾ in.

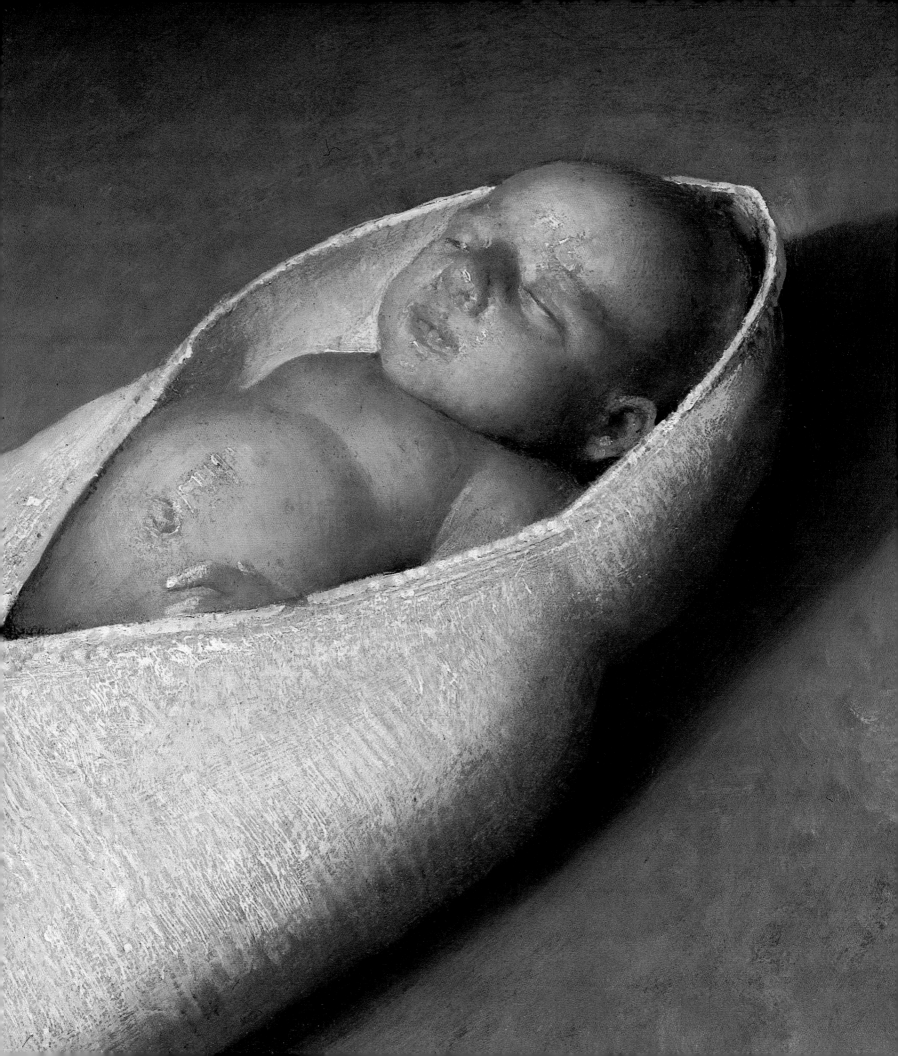

**91.** *Baby in Deserted Landscape*, 1995–96. 35 ½ x 38 ¼ in.

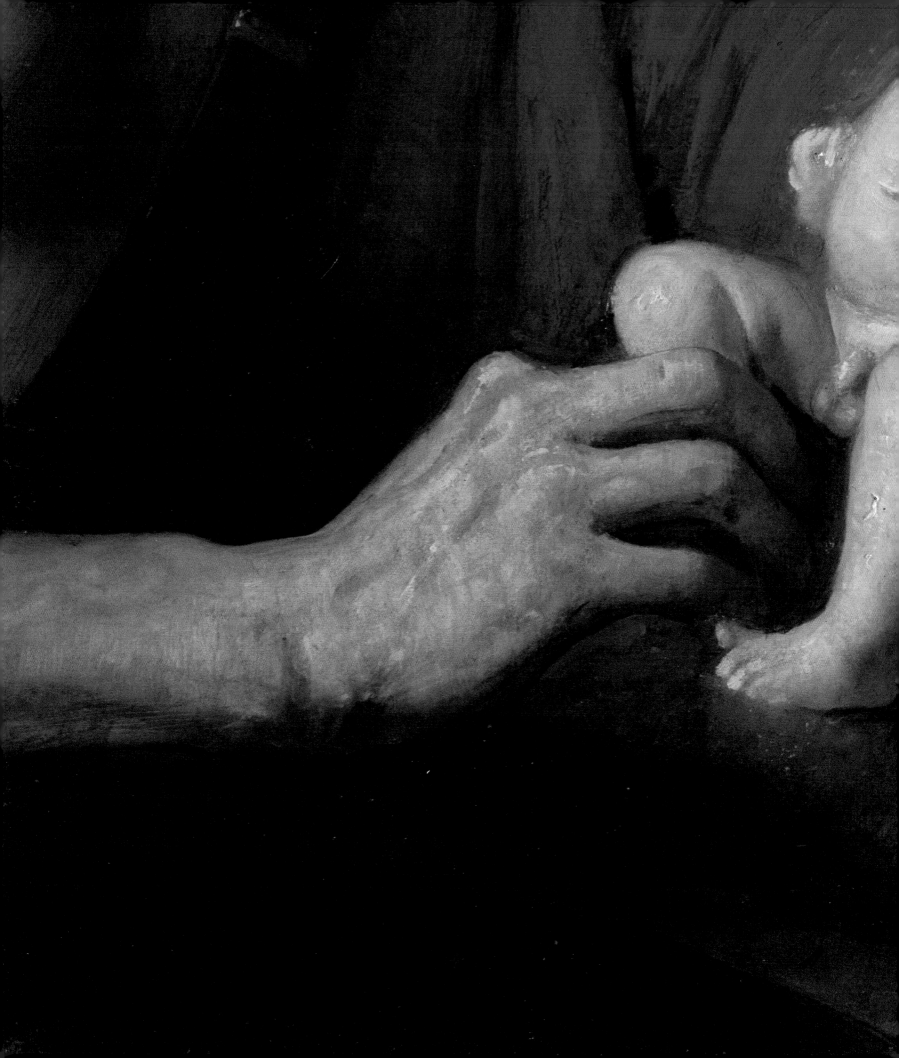

**92.** *The Lifesaver,* 1995–96. 59 x 45 ¼ in.

above the natural baptismal font. The lantern has been extinguished, and behind the baby looms the broken columnar cliff. From the triangular mountain fire is leaking into the darkness. In *Barter* (93) there are, however, no straight forms in the rocky forest spreading behind the stage where a woman is offering her breast to a wandering warrior. It is not known what Nerdrum may have meant by these strange Icelandic rock formations, but no doubt they carried some significance. The armed man has an amulet hanging from his hair, the way the *Woman with Fish* did, while the reddish brown fur waistcoat matches the color of the clothes in *Five Namegivers*. On his shoulder he carries a bundle of unknown significance, but he is apparently a person searching for love. The woman, whom Nerdrum in conversation called «agrarian,» has a plain, golden wrap and seemingly plays a similar role as the woman exposing her breast in *Five Persons around a Water Hole*. Even if one cannot determine the concrete origin of the painting, it might make sense to regard the couple as contributing to the visualization of an ideal state in the world of Odd Nerdrum, where people think with their bodies and act according to their more basic needs, and where concepts like care and warmth are an even trade for protection and strength.

The development of Nerdrum's self-image took an interesting turn in 1995. After displaying his tired, but determined face in *Frontal Self-Portrait* (94), he started painting a Norwegian national hero, Cato Zahl Pedersen, calling it *Unarmed Man* (95). This was a man Nerdrum respected. At a young age an accident had seriously maimed him, but with an iron will and strict discipline he had managed to conquer his fate, becoming not only a champion in the Paralympics, but also completing the physically and mentally challenging expedition «Unarmed to the South Pole.» But Nerdrum obviously speaks as much of himself as he does of this man's well-trained body. Asked about his strong attraction to amputated bodies in connection with this picture, he replied: «I suppose all situations are about self-identification. In a way we are all handicapped.»[25] Compared to his earlier self-portrayals as an amputee, the focus has moved from the victim or the loser to the winner, the scarred victor. This is signaled through the animal hide, a reference to the Hercules myth, lying across the steel chair and testifying to the one who conquered danger

and evil. Conspicuously placed on the floor lies a rope with a small reddish plume of victory, a symbol also worn in *Buried Alive* (96), in which Nerdrum returns once again to the scene of the great betrayal. In this exorcism scene he is wearing a helmet that has one strap hanging limp like a donkey's ear, while the other stands up like a powerful wing of victory. He has put down his gun and is frantically digging a hole in the bloodred earth in order to finally bring his mourning to an end. The living body he is about to dump is contorted in fear and is one of the most hideous creatures ever painted by Nerdrum. To emphasize her repulsiveness he has pierced her nose – in the visual vocabulary of Odd Nerdrum he demonstrates that «being modern – is disgusting.»[26] Night has fallen on the landscape, giving it a tinge of the bluish color of a vein. At the foot of the triangular mountain in the distance their one-time home is burning. But up on the hill a stone arch stands as an entry portal into a new landscape, indicating that his long rite of passage was drawing to a close.

Meanwhile Nerdrum had acquired another, more public problem, to deal with. Together with the sculptor Per Ung he had for years criticized the National Academy of Art for their failure to teach classical figurative techniques. In the summer of 1988 five of his former pupils, together with three other young artists, wrote an open letter to the ministry, demanding that something be done.[27] Nothing happened until the fall of 1994. By then this writer had become head of the Academy, and I now proposed two new professorships in figurative art. All hell broke loose. Staff and students alike protested vociferously against the idea, internally as well as in the media. Being a natural candidate for such a position, Nerdrum was drawn into the fray – first as a heartily scorned old-masterly painter, subsequently as a despised person. Following a year of turmoil the minister of education, Gudmund Hernes, was able to get both the professorships and the necessary funding to carry out the idea. Hell broke loose again.

Everyone knew that if Nerdrum applied for the position in painting, he would get it. In the opinion of the Nordic professional committee that later evaluated the candidates he had no competitors, being «in a class of his own,» also in terms of the international art scene.[28] The resistance at the Academy, as well as in parts of Norwegian society, now escalated to hysteria.[29] And at the end of

**93.** *Barter,* 1995–96. 71 x 82 ¾ in.

**94.** *Frontal Self-Portrait,* 1994–95. 29 ½ x 23 ¾ in.

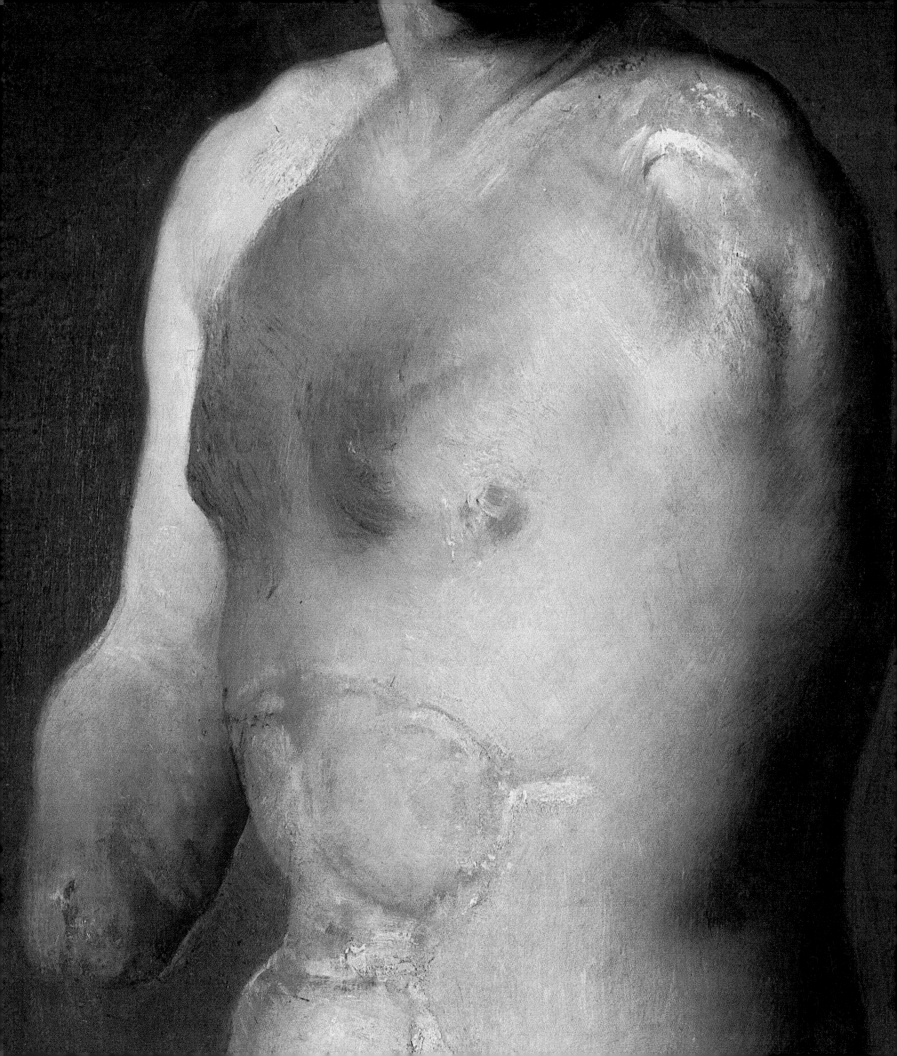

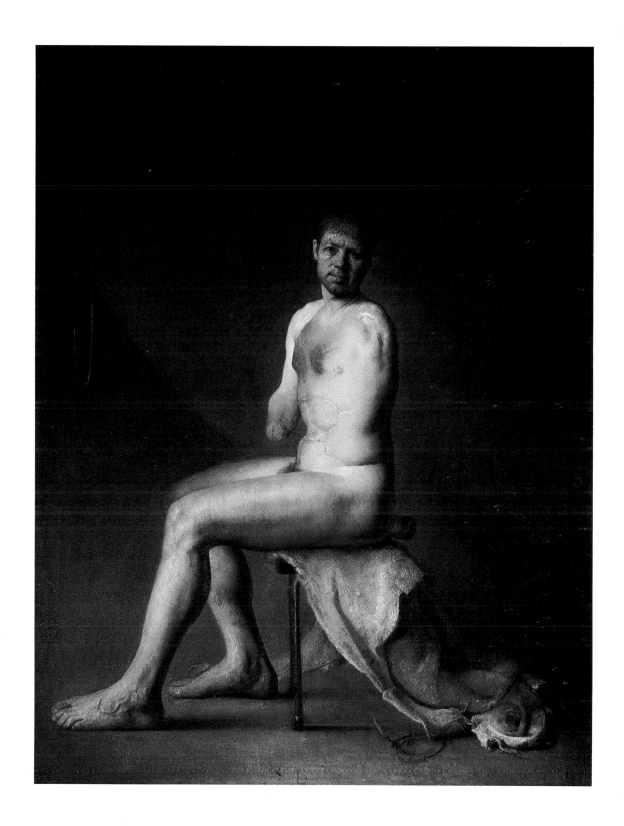

**95.** *Unarmed Man,* 1995. 72 x 66 in.

1995, when Nerdrum decided to apply for the position, there was a storm of protests against him, which finally made him withdraw his application on 20 June 1996, the day before his appointment.[30] Two days earlier *Dagbladet*, the tabloid that is Norway's third largest newspaper, printed an editorial that must be exceptional even in Norwegian cultural history, especially seen from an artist's point of view. Starting with a clarification of an earlier editorial 15 June, thereby launching the paper's official protest against the appointment of Nerdrum, it concluded:

*Let it be said: Norwegian art ought to find room for many forms of expression, also Odd Nerdrum's. But we do not believe that he represents the future of Norwegian art, either at the Academy or anywhere else.*[31]

One may well speculate on the conditions and ideas that made it imperative to editorialize on the permissibility of painting like Odd Nerdrum in Norway. But a more relevant question concerns the impact on Nerdrum of having a leading newspaper in his native country openly refuse him all future possibilities on his home turf. For this message did not come from an irritated journalist or an agitated art critic. It came from the heart of the newspaper.

By now Nerdrum had already donned his armor in a self-portrait begun at the end of 1995 (97). When he first showed this painting, at an exhibition in Stockholm in May 1996, he called it *Old Warrior*, opening for another level of meaning. The gleaming, golden breastplate represents not only a considerable part of the self-image of a man who has used his art to fight the psychological battle taking place behind his own outer shell, or, as he had earlier observed: «Much of the best in art deals with rejection – of overcoming the pain inflicted on the self-revealer by the community of others.»[32] The baroque armor also signifies the champion of art, who, like a Marco Polo of painting, had rediscovered a forgotten continent, spending a lifetime fighting to have it accepted as valid art. With provocative statements like: «I know I'm destroying the new with the old» and anti-modern attitudes, such as regarding it as a mark of quality to stagnate in deep absorption, he has also had ample reason to defend himself against counterattacks.[33] Especially in the nineties, when

he has time and again claimed that the ideological fundamentalism and excluding persecution of divergent art forms that mark prevailing in contemporary art has had much too clear parallels in the authoritarian systems of nazism and communism. And yet, maybe it is the *Stripper* (98), a painting he began working on towards the end of the academic imbroglio, that best illustrates his vision of the kind of survival strategy he had to choose in adversity. Flanked by two rather ominous-looking characters, the left one wearing the fox skin that signifies cleverness and wile, the old man has dropped his pale red cloth and, in the manner of Hamlet, turned himself into an innocuous clown in a crazy St. Vitus' dance. Nerdrum could hardly have painted a clearer image of himself as too radical for his time, especially to an academy so preoccupied with keeping up with the latest international trends in mainstream contemporary art. It may have been the enormous relief he felt at finally escaping that hysterical hornets' nest he revealed in the technically very Titian-inspired self-portrait *Hepatitis* (99). Both the title and the unusual interior had their origin in a lengthy hospital stay in 1972 because of a jaundice infection. In this painting he has depicted the hazy, euphoric state of happiness he experienced once the overwhelming fatigue lifted.[34] There is no doubt that he had been under great pressure ever since the fall of 1995, partly to apply for the position and to publicly fight the entire appointment battle, but also partly due to the prospect of six years of internal strife in a hopeless public institution where he was unwanted. He has scarcely mentioned this situation in conversations; but a couple of years earlier, when I asked the stupid question if he was ever happy, he gave this answer:

*For that I would first have to forget my experiences. They loom like a dark cloud over the whole situation. I am weighed down by the memories. They never go away. I have experienced things that have paralyzed me mentally; and I never experience true happiness, that is, the happiness that means an absence of longing and an unawareness of evil. The only happiness I can feel is when I can get away from society and its demands. Then there is a kind of feeling of freedom. Happiness is escaping, being set free.*[35]

**96.** *Buried Alive,* 1995–96. 43 ¼ x 45 ¼ in.

**98.** *Stripper,* 1996. 81 x 101 ¼ in.

97. *Self-Portrait in Armor,* 1995–96. 39 x 33 ¾ in.

**99.** *Hepatitis*, 1996 – 97. 80 x 75 ½ in.

In *Dancer with Snake* (100) Nerdrum has shown how he sees himself positioned in relation to international competitors in figurative painting. This writer again feels some responsibility for this turning up as a subject Nerdrum needed to paint. In the fall of 1995 I took the initiative to organize an exhibition in which Odd Nerdrum would meet the artist who, along with himself, identified most closely with the great art of the past in his work – the Italian Carlo Maria Mariani, whom I had introduced in Norway in 1990, both in an exhibition as well as in a comprehensive catalogue text.[36] Nerdrum did not meet his colleague at the time, but he knew of him and had read the article. The exhibition now being planned, carried the title *The Ideal and the Real* and was intended to counterpoise two different kinds of «dissidents» in late twentieth-century art.[37] For Mariani is also very critical to conventional contemporary art, but his visual basis is located in a different art-historical tradition. His point of reference is classicism from ancient Greece through the Renaissance, especially Neoclassicism at the end of the eighteenth century. Unlike Nerdrum, Mariani is not interested in natural substances and does not stress the importance of using old master painting techniques. He considers himself a conceptual painter, instead imitating ideas and concepts in his work, especially the long discarded classicist concept of Beauty. Nerdrum was still looking forward to meet Mariani, so that he could compare his paintings and ideals with his own. All winter he had pondered over the catalogue text I had prepared, in which the positions of the two artists were initially presented in these words:

*An apt visual metaphor that illustrates some of their personal positions in terms of style and aesthetic anchoring may be found in Raphael's* School of Athens. *Here Plato and Aristotle are standing at the center of antiquity's philosophical scene, giving their signs for everything that has subsequently been associated with idealism and realism in both art and thought. Plato raises his hand, pointing to the realm of ideas as the basis for understanding reality, as Mariani also feels that ideas and idealized classicist forms of expression are always more beautiful than nature. Aristotle, on the other hand, stretches out his hand above the ground as an indication that reality itself is both the origin and the test of our ideas, as Nerdrum also seeks his old-masterly-formed ideals of beauty in nature's most basic appearances.*

In March 1996, less than a month before the exhibition was to open, uncertainty arose concerning Mariani's participation, and the whole project was cancelled. The catalogue was never printed, and Nerdrum had to hurriedly find another partner for the Stockholm exhibition.[38] A couple of months later he began to work on two paintings that appear to be related to this incident and his reflections on it.

Looking at *Dancer with Snake*, it is not readily apparent that this is some sort of a wasteland *School of Athens*, in which Nerdrum confronts Mariani the way Aristotle confronted Plato in Raphael's painting. It then helps to remember that Nerdrum does not paint factual, «objective» situations. His visions and coded visual images are very subjective entities and reflect only his own experiences and perceptions of himself in particular contexts. In this case he has made himself into a wild hermit, arriving in a boat to challenge the man in the protective bastion. The slim, unkempt dancer has put his staff down on the ground and holds up the snake he has brought along as a threat to the well-fed inhabitant. The visitor points to the ground, but is on his way to the sky. The other, more static figure points upwards, but is weighed down to the ground by his huge body. He has partly hidden himself behind the windbreak and holds a knife behind his back. From the sky he has caught a raven, now hanging dead in his dwelling. The grand helmet may together with the amulet recall the accessories of *Woman with Fish*, and was probably meant to be of a more general significance, so that only the raven relates directly to Mariani. Nerdrum was well aware that Mariani had painted a raven as an attribute to Jannis Kounellis in his large allegory of the contemporary *School of Rome*, shown in 1982 at Documenta in Kassel.[39] But Nerdrum also knew that his views were diametrically opposed to those of Mariani in the question of whether nature or idea was the origin of Beauty. In a speech he wrote in 1988 Nerdrum had been very clear concerning his own art: «The renewing factor lies hidden in nature, not in the ideas about nature.»[40] And this is the situation he has depicted in *Dancer with Snake*. He did not himself connect the raven to Apollo but rather to the Norse warrior god Odin, who, tall, bearded, and one-eyed had traded his other eye for wisdom. The snake in the picture is also used as a sign of natural wisdom. Nor had it been an exclusively

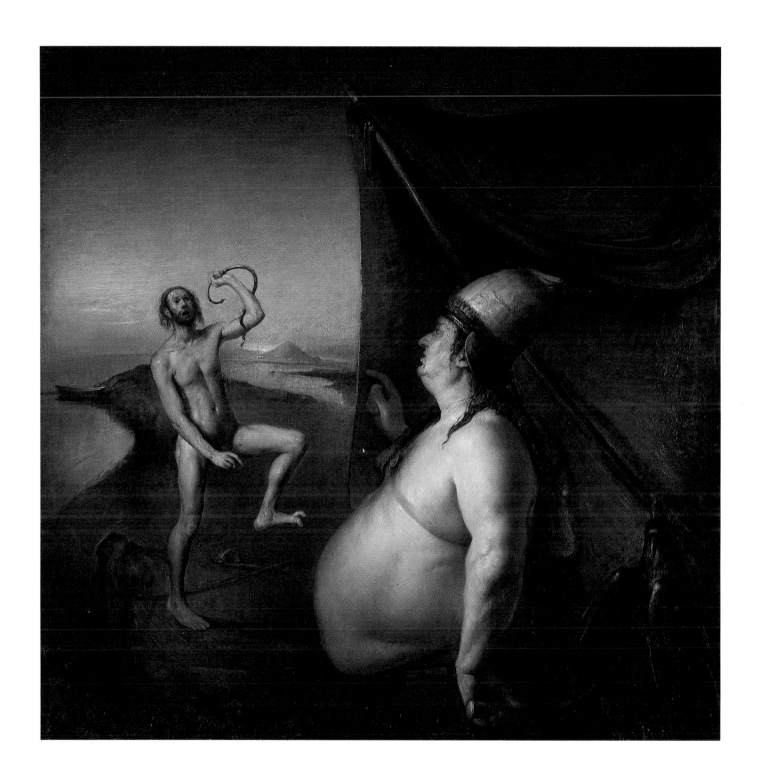

**100.** *Dancer with Snake,* 1996. 68 x 70 in.

negative feature in his other paintings, as the one in *Man Bitten by a Snake* brings about a moment of realization, in which the subconscious speaks its wordless warning long before the bitter experience of reality makes wise. And in *Man with a Woman's Head* the snake was also a symbol of the brutal force of nature blindly guiding some fatal human actions. Nerdrum was, in other words, eager to show that his ideal was the material and earthbound realities and that it was the profane that was to be sacralized.

The other painting that can be seen as related to Nerdrum's reflections in connection with the scheduled meeting with Mariani is *Boy with Icon* (101), for here he seems to have depicted his notion of an earthly ideal of beauty, by his portrayal of an uninjured and very sensual young man. His primitive fur is elegantly draped, and the piece of cloth wrapped around his beautiful head is delicately arranged in rounded, resting forms. In his clenched hand he holds a talisman-like sculpture, and his staff has a small buckhorn handle. One might have expected the background curtain to darken the landscape and leave nothing but a solitary triangular mountain. But the intention may be quite the opposite. In conversation Nerdrum has indicated that he saw the statuette as a Greco-Roman figure, which in his case would point in two different directions. In part it would then refer to a rational and civilizing factor, and consequently to a destructive element in his nameless world, as the mountain might suggest. But

the statuette may also signify pre-Christian values, seen by Nerdrum as wholly positive in art, thought, and life in general. In addition, when he is apparently able to conceive of himself as taking on an Aristotelian role, there is a ready parallel to Rembrandt's *Aristotle Contemplating a Bust of Homer* – the blind storyteller (fig.). Hence he did not want to obstruct the view but instead allow his interior to open up into the timeless landscape of the refuge, the same way Rembrandt let the world of books appear behind the curtains in his painting. In this context the ambiguous buckhorn with its «evil» point becomes a reference to a Dionysian element in Nerdrum's aesthetics – complete hedonism, in which the sensual realities of life lived are always more beautiful than cerebral ideals.

In *The Nightjumper* (102) he indicates that idealism in its Christian derivation also may appear as a negative concept in his imagery. Just like *Dancer with Snake* the painting is divided into two equal parts. On the left is a man defecating high up on a mountainside. He is placed in a relaxed and natural state of happiness, witnessing the giant jump performed by the figure down on the ground before the symbolic trinity of the razor-sharp mountain peak. The jumper has his base amidst four sleeping figures lying in the same circular formation as in *The Night Guard* (30), where the «aberrant» served as night watchman of the world, guarding his right to be different. The jumper has now taken over his position, for here we find the staff and the metal canteen used in *Revier* (31). Aside from «The Loveknife,» Nerdrum included only one single aphoristic concept in his *Notater*, and that was *The Nightjumper*.[41] In conversation he indicated that this represented himself, who in the turbulent period around 1990–91 had such strong nightmares and anxiety attacks that he virtually jumped in his sleep. In the painting he has contrasted his mental pain and anguish from that time with his current state of more earthbound well-being, self-contentedly pointing to himself as he rids himself of his bodily burden. The attributes he still carries like shackles also give a clear signal that he has had a special woman in mind: the golden cloth belt and the deep-red, heart-shaped velvet bag of sweet memories, contrasted with the painful knife and the destructive gold cross.[42] And finally, it is apparent that in the magnificently painted back he has used a much more classicist technique of fine-painting than he usually

Rembrandt: *Aristotle Contemplating a Bust of Homer,* 1653. Metropolitan Museum of Art, New York.

**101.** *Boy with Icon,* 1996. 47 x 40 ½ in.

does, maybe a special code for the ambivalence that still riddled his psyche: Odiosanto – the love-hate of the beautiful and sensuous nature, betraying life for sensible ideals.

The psychological processing of his six-year-old love loss also constituted a major feature of his work in 1997. In *Initiation* (103) he resumes where he left off in *Hermaphrodite*, where the couple was resurrected in gold, and in the significance of the stone arch in *Buried Alive*. The mood in this picture is far more positive, since the sharp peaks have been replaced by a massively resting fort in the opening. It is also noticeable that the aspect of a final union of the couple has been more clearly defined, since the golden-clad androgyne is as much man as woman. On either side stand figures, identifiable as Nerdrum's former lover on the right and himself on the left, the latter hand-in-hand with his un-natural principle of unification. A pale, barren young woman is stopped from introducing the twig of the female figure in *Blind Wanderer* into the group, while an elderly love-seeking female wanderer watches them with her lantern lit. Nerdrum's continued preoccupation with his heartache is also visible in *Man with Long Hair* (104), in which the eye-injured, harelipped wanderer has gotten the girl's curly hair from *Woman Killing Injured Man*. The staff has been replaced by a protective bronze shield, and on his hand sits his slender little companion, twittering. On the horizon there is a factory smokestack, and below in the dark is the faint outline of a boat, in which «life floats on the black sea of death – alone.»[43] *Old Man with Dead Maiden* (105) openly reveals the legacy of having to tow along a living dead on his mental plains. One-eyed, dissolved, and weakened, he almost pleads for release. Perhaps his plea was heard, for in *Pissing Woman* (106), which he began working on towards the end of the year, his former lover no longer plays the lead. A plump female body with no legs, arms, and teeth lies in a grayish landscape of nasty little peaks of lava. Someone has also been towing this woman through life, most likely the amputated man standing in front of his house, breaking the horizon with his arm held high in a greeting of the morning light. The dog – which must be of great significance, since Nerdrum had never before painted such an animal – shows its red tongue, while lustfully eyeing the peeing cripple, a woman incapable of rising by her own power. This is no doubt the closest Nerdrum has ever come to the

American photographer Joel-Peter Witkin's macabre expositions of amputees. Unlike the *Unarmed Man*, whom Nerdrum had painted a couple of years earlier, there is reason to believe that none of the persons serving as models or inspiration for this painting had been maimed. It would be very risky to suggest any «embarrassingly concrete» reason for the problems addressed here. But in regard to his «innermost thoughts» coming to the fore, one might bear in mind his comments shortly after finishing this painting: «The ideas are often insane visions that I go on to put into a human context . . . When I start working, there is often some local meanness in the picture; but as I keep on working, I force it out of the local towards an eternal, universal image – a transformation.»[44] There is still the question of how far into eternity he has been able to force his vision.

When Nerdrum rose from his sickbed in *Hepatitis*, there were also signs that his lengthy convalescence from the traumatic love-loss had entered a new phase. In the summer of 1997 he finally reported his regained health in a series of bright and airy summer paintings, in which he depicted settings and motifs he had not painted for the previous thirteen years. Some of the images still included metaphoric signs of old anguish, as, for example, the eel in *Woman Resting on a Rock* (107) and the exposed baby in *Mother with Child* (108), but the clear sky and the clean, white dress were for the first time allowed to overpower Nerdrum's dark, melancholy look in the brilliant *Blue Self-Portrait* (109). Towards the end of the year there was an incident that brought Nerdrum back to the gold in his own veins and made him king in his own kingdom once again. One evening in early December 1997, he was seeing some guests out; and, standing on the front steps of his house, he saw her waiting in the dark outside the gate. According to him their conversation was brief but clearly indicated to him that she wanted to continue. Shortly afterwards he decided how to render his next self-portrait (110). First he had a gown made, in a golden brocade studded with white pearls. Next he stood in front of the mirror in his studio, alone, giving the most private rendering imaginable of how the vitality and virility that had been lost in the form of the dry twig in *Blind Wanderer* was now fully restored. The earth-colored backdrop curtain is draped similarly to the one in the 1985 *Anine* portrait, and on the left Nerdrum has placed a crimson-colored bundle of cloth in the shape

102. *The Nightjumper*, 1996. 67 ¾ x 67 ¾ in.

103. *Initiation,* 1997. 81 ½ x 104  in.

104. *Man with Long Hair*, 1997. 67 x 43 ¼ in.

105. *Old Man with Dead Maiden*, 1997. 81 ½ x 98 ¾ in.

106. *Pissing Woman*, 1997–98. 80 ¾ x 99 ¼ in.

**107.** *Woman Resting on a Rock,* 1997. 59 x 59 in.

108. *Mother with Child*, 1997. 27 ½ x 39 ¼ in.

**109.** *Blue Self-Portrait,* 1997. 43 x 37 ¾ in.

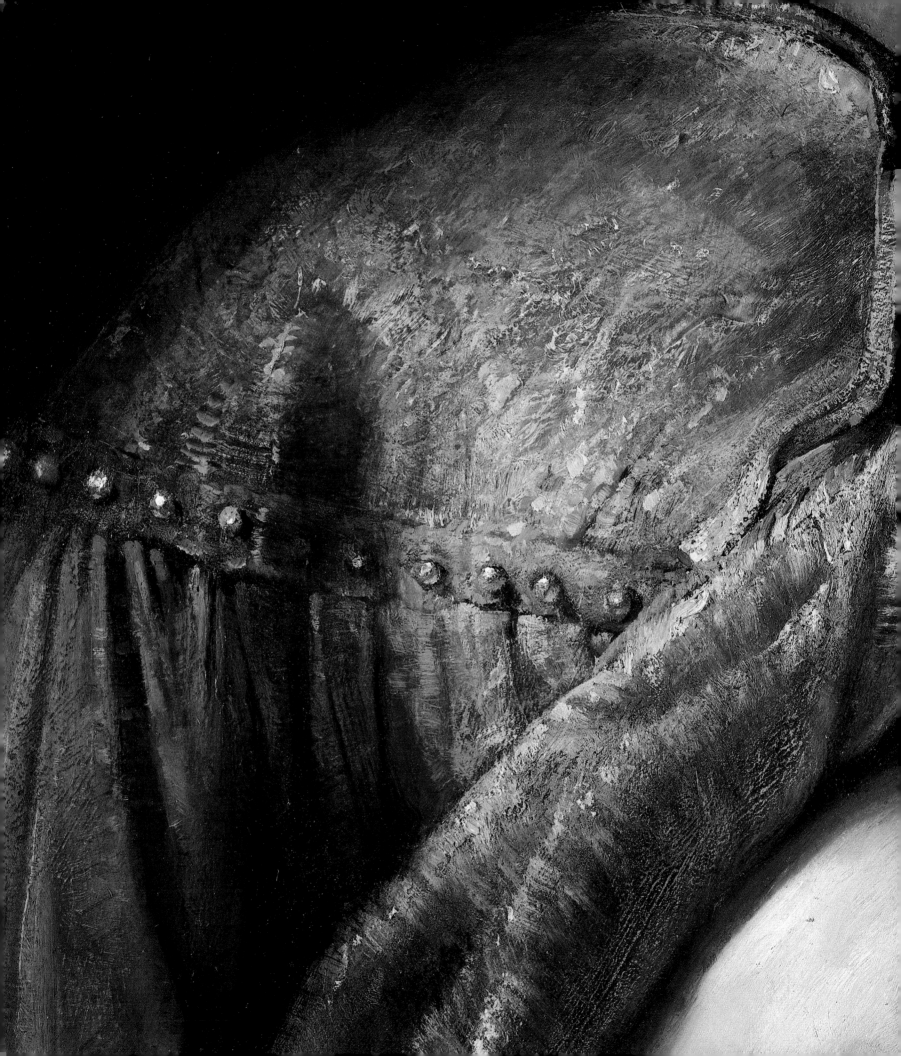

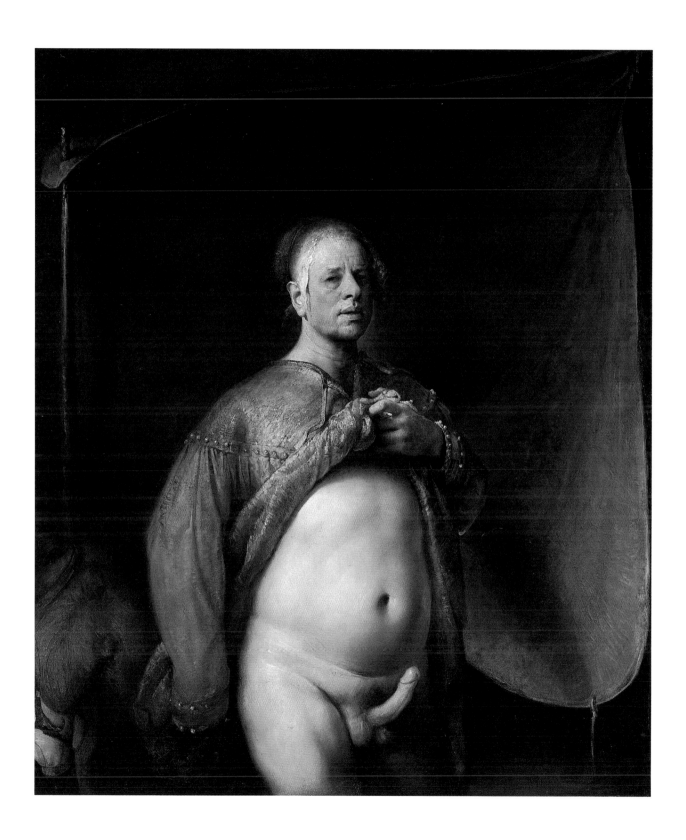

**110.** *Self-Portrait in Golden Gown,* 1998. 73 ¾ x 56 ¾ in.

of a warm, soft behind. From the pole hangs a leather belt ending in a sharp claw resting against the sleeve of a light red cape. He has put up his hair to imitate the shape of the woman's head in the portrait, and there is every indication that the baroque sun king can now celebrate the great moment of triumph. But his eyes do not quite join in the celebration. Instead they are filled with quiet woe. The importance of this look was indicated in Nerdrum's quoting Schopenhauer: «Why do lovers look at one another with such sadness in their eyes?»[45] And the same very human factor that once contributed to his own conception rose again here in all its old-masterly abundance to retell the old story. The cycle was complete, but in his own case, fruitlessly completed.

*   *   *

At the time he was showing his summer paintings, and only a few days before he got his idea for the unusual self-portrait, Nerdrum also launched his new and quite provocative label for himself: «king of kitsch.»[46] After many years of competing on an international art scene that would never understand the importance of his undertaking or recognize his achievement within the area that meant something to him, namely the skills of the old masters in rendering human flesh and other textures, he simply resigned from the high society of art. He had long observed his fellow figurative artists, in their nearly frantic fear of not being art-politically correct, deny the validity of the art forms of the past, and, above all, distance themselves from the dreaded concept of kitsch. Now he seized the bull by the horns and openly declared that he had nothing in common with the concept of art as used in our own century. Armed with his new understanding of kitsch, he named himself the representative of a totally different paradigm, in which his entire enterprise was a foreign body within the prevailing art establishment. His own kitsch and the art of the others were two separate worlds, existing side by side in parallel universes. Only now did he realize that all those who had for years accused him of being engaged in nothing but sentimental kitsch had been right: «I have painted kitsch all along; I have never been an artist . . . I now apologize for having imposed on art, of operating under false pretenses. But I did not know what I was doing.»[47]

Nerdrum's concept of kitsch is a personal construction, reflecting his own enterprise and understanding of himself. Although some of his views can be seen as related to a reverse reading of the writings on kitsch by, for instance, Hermann Broch and Milan Kundera, his approach is a very different one.[48] Nerdrum sees the concepts of art and kitsch as having reversed their roles since the end of the nineteenth century. Starting with Cezanne, the modernists transformed art into an exercise in pure design and became the «timekeepers of science,» in Nerdrum's words. Kitsch then came to mean everything else that still dealt with sensuality and emotion, as the art of the past had once done. Were Rembrandt alive today, he would be considered kitsch, according to Nerdrum. Thus he disagrees with Kundera, who claims that the ideal of cleanliness and the denial of the body that first characterized

the term kitsch, when it appeared in the middle of «the sentimental nineteenth century,» is still valid: «kitsch is the absolute denial of shit, in both the literal and the figurative senses
of the word; kitsch excludes everything from its purview
which is essentially unacceptable in human existence.»[49] On
the contrary, says Nerdrum. In his definition of kitsch nothing genuinely human is unacceptable and no feelings prohibited. Kitsch, unlike art, has no restrictions. It does not fear
art as art fears kitsch. It exists solely by virtue of a basic human need for expression, not for the suppression of that
which is called art. Kitsch serves life, while art serves itself.
Thus kitsch is not authoritarian in nature. Instead art has in-
herited the cerebral ideals of the original kitsch, its denial of
sensuality and its efforts to be in line with public «truth.»
Today it is art that seeks «cleanliness» and «authenticity,» not
the kitsch, since the genuine and poignant emotions it strives
to express might better be described as turbid and fraudu-
lent: «Kitsch has nothing to do with truth. It is the domain
of aesthetics and the beautiful lie.»[50] It also does not address
the public in general, the way art does, but instead speaks directly to the individual. That is why kitsch is not concerned
with innovation or originality or even with its place in a linear understanding of history, something Nerdrum had
touched upon in one of his aphorisms, when he urged: «Go
backwards into the future, so that your face is lit up by the
past.»[51] Kitsch, according to him, disregards art's moral cove-
nant with society, being instead a celebration of the individual's private desires, or what he most needs to express. But
there is no room for irony, for kitsch is based on the utmost
sincerity. The kitsch painter seeks to create something so
vitally convincing in terms of emotion that other individuals
are moved by it, and he cannot understand why intellectuals
only laugh, while he himself is crying. Unlike art, kitsch is
therefore not a random choice in life. As in the case of Nerdrum, one is «stricken by a talent,» and thus victim to an
overpowering need to imitate that nature in which the timelessly human can shine. All that matters is that one does it
as well as it has been done before – in his case by the old
masters. Then there is no excuse in having been born in the
twentieth century.

In this respect Odd Nerdrum may very well be right when he
says that he can only be «The Savior of Painting» as the king
of kitsch.

111. *Twins* 1998. 74 ¾ x 100 ¾ in.

112. *Night-Light,* 1981–98. 35 x 30 in.

113. *Self-Portrait in Profile*, 1998. 33 ½ x 30 ½ in.

# NOTES

## OLD MASTER IDEALS

1  His mother confirmed this to the newspaper *Verdens Gang* on 30 November 1996: «During his teens he felt that something was wrong… He had the feeling that the father he had grown up with – was not his father. I kept it a secret for all those years to protect everyone…» A good deal of personal information about Nerdrum may also be found in Jan-Erik Ebbestad Hansen's biography *Fenomenet Nerdrum* [The Nerdrum Phenomenon] (Oslo: Gyldendal, 1996).

2  *Verdens Gang*, 25 September 1997.

3  Taped conversation, 25 January 1998.

4  Ibid.

5  *Morgenposten*, 25 November 1967.

6  Unpublished speech at Drammen kunstforening, December 1987.

7  Taped conversation, 25 January 1998.

8  *Aftenposten*, 18 February 1996.

9  Pål Hougen, in *Dagbladet*, 24 June 1964.

10  Ole Henrik Moe, in *Aftenposten*, 11 June 1964.

11  The phrase was coined by Hans-Jacob Brun in *Dagbladet*, 30 November 1967.

12  *Arbeiderbladet*, 28 November 1987.

13  Quoted from Mikael Wivel, «Et norsk fenomen» [A Norwegian phenomenon], *Information*, 18 January 1977.

14  *Morgenbladet*, 8 November 1980.

15  Quoted from a conversation in New York, September 1987.

16  Robert Meyer: «Odd Nerdrum i New York i 1968.» *Samtiden* 2 (1990): p.42.

17  *Aftenposten*, 29 April 1972.

18  «'Det rasjonelle' og kunsten» [The rational and art], *Aftenposten*, 10 June 1972.

19  Andries Pels, quoted by Christopher Brown in: *Rembrandt* (Rizzoli, 1979), p. 3.

20  William Blake, *Jerusalem*, II, 36 (1804-1820). In Nerdrum's collection of aphorisms, *Notater* (Oslo: Aschehoug, 1992), p. 29, he made his own version of Blake's line: «Consciousness Stands between the Subconscious and Something Unknown.»

21  Hans Richter: *DADA: Art and Anti-Art* (London: Thames and Hudson, 1965), p. 64.

22  *Dagbladet*, 15 November 1967.

23  *Morgenposten*, 25 November 1967.

24  Arild Haaland, ed., *Odd Nerdrum: Bilder* (Oslo: Tanum-Norli, 1983), p. 139.

25  *Bergens Tidende*, 28 May 1971.

26  Haaland, *Odd Nerdrum*, p. 142.

27  *Dagbladet*, 15 November 1967.

28  *Aftenposten*, 18 February 1996.

29  Charles Baudelaire, *Curiosités esthetiques: L'art romantique* (Paris: Garnier, 1962), p. 672.

30  Audun Engh, «Odd Nerdrum: Jeg tror på åndskapitalisme.'» [Odd Nerdrum: 'I believe in a capitalism of the mind'] Interview in *Gateavisa* 2 (1985), p. 8.

31  Jean-Paul Sartre, *Being and Nothingness* (New York: 1965), p. 140.

32  Ibid.

33  Homer, *Odyssey* 9.105.

34  Haaland, *Odd Nerdrum*, p.139.

35  *Alle menn* (1982).

36  Haaland, *Odd Nerdrum*, p. 140.

37  *Aftenposten*, 28 September 1985.

38  *Alle menn* (1982).

39  Götz Adriani, Winfried Konnertz, and Karin Thomas, *Joseph Beuys: Life and Works* (New York: Barron's, 1979), p. 2.

40  Quoted from Ronald Feldman in a conversation in New York, September 1987.

## THE MENTAL REFUGE

1  Engh, «Odd Nerdrum,» p. 11. There is only one version of *Dentures*, while the brick has been painted in four versions: red in 1982, pink in 1983, and white in 1984 and 1998.

2  Ibid.

3  Odd Nerdrum has three daughters by his former companion, Cecilie Knudsen: Nora (1978), Oda (1982), and Amo (1984). He has two sons by his current wife, Turid Spildo: Bork (1993) and Øde (1995). The latter name means «deserted.»

4  Engh, «Odd Nerdrum,» p. 13. The quote in the next sentence is taken from page 12.

5  Jan Åke Pettersson, «Odd Nerdrum: Evighetens synsvinkel» [Odd Nerdrum: From the eternal point of view]. Interview in *Siksi: the Nordic Art Review* 1 (1987): p. 17. Here Nerdrum also elaborates on his concept of substance.

6  *Aftenposten*, 28 September 1985.

7  *Verdens Gang*, 1 November 1984. His *Isola* model was his former student Trine Folmoe.

8  Seneferu Semb's reserve-head in the Cairo Museum.

9  Engh, «Odd Nerdrum,» p. 12.

10  The 1968 version of *Man in Abandoned Landscape* has been reversed on the cover of Odd Jan Sandsdalen's poetry collection *Det står en regnboge spent* (Oslo: Dreyer, 1981).

11  *Verdens Gang*, 1 November 1984.

12  Pettersson, «Odd Nerdrum: Evighetens synsvinkel,» p. 16.

13  Engh, «Odd Nerdrum,» p. 6.

14  Ibid., p. 12.

15  Ibid., p. 11.

16  Pettersson, «Odd Nerdrum: Evighetens synsvinkel,» p. 14. The Norwegian artist Frans Widerberg started using this curved landscape with his hovering figures as early as the seventies.

17  Immanuel Kant, *Critique of Judgement* (1790), § 26-30.

18  Pettersson, «Odd Nerdrum: Evighetens synsvinkel,» p. 17.

19  The phrase is taken from Karin Blehr's article «Bedrag og behag» [Deceit and pleasure], in *Natur og kultur* 3 (1983).

20  *Bergens Tidende*, 17 November 1984.

21  See: Julian Jaynes, *The Origin of Consciousness in the Breakdown of the Bicameral Mind* (Boston: Houghton Mifflin, 1976), p. 299-300. See also: Alfred Guillaume, *Prophecy and Divination among the Hebrews and other Semites* (London: Hodder and Stoughton, 1938).

22  Eccleasiastes 1:2, 7:25.

23  Zechariah 13:3-4.

24  Homer *Odyssey* 8.500.

25  Ibid., 8.64.

26  Engh, «Odd Nerdrum,» p. 10.

27  *Dagbladet*, 1 November 1984.

28  Pettersson, «Odd Nerdrum: Evighetens synsvinkel,» p. 16.

29  Ibid., p. 16. This is Nerdrum's own description.

30  Ibid.

31  Unpublished manuscript for a lecture tour of the U.S., 2-10 November 1988: New Jersey, San Francisco, and Madison, Wisconsin.

32  Nerdrum has stated that he did not see these films until 1987 and that they are hardly relevant to his imagery or thinking.

33  *Aftenposten*, 20 August 1988.

34  *Dagbladet*, 14 January 1989.

35  Taped conversation, 25 January 1998.

36  *Upp & Ner* (Stockholm) 9 (1990), p.55-56.

37  At the beginning of *Mysteries* Knut Hamsun tells the story of a man who has committed suicide because of a broken heart and has been found «lying on his stomach with his face in a puddle.» In a lecture at Drammen kunstforening in 1987 Nerdrum himself reported that the idea for *Sole Morte* came from a dream in which the financier-publisher Trygve Hegnar – who had also served as a model for the murderer in the Baader painting – insisted that the artist climb his latest acquisition: a tall tower of earth with a spiral ramp strewn with white marble gravel leading around the outside to the top. When Nerdrum got there, he found himself staring into the unblinking eyes of a Sami standing in a small but deep water hole. Only when Nerdrum noticed that the water reached the man's nose, did he realize that the eyes meeting his were dead. It is unclear, however, whether the painting represents a retelling of the content of the dream.

38  Pettersson, «Odd Nerdrum: Evighetens synsvinkel,» p. 17.

39  Taped conversation, 30 March 1994.

40  Engh, «Odd Nerdrum,» p. 5 and Pettersson, «Odd Nerdrum: Evighetens synsvinkel,» p. 13.

41  Pettersson, «Odd Nerdrum: Evighetens synsvinkel,» p. 17.

42  *Dine penger* 5 (1992), p. 38.

43  Pettersson, «Odd Nerdrum: Evighetens synsvinkel,» p. 18.

44  Engh, «Odd Nerdrum,» p. 12.

45  *Arbeiderbladet*, 28 November 1987.

46  Odd Nerdrum, *Notater* (Oslo: Aschehoug, 1992), p. 86.

47 See, e.g., interviews in *Aftenposten,* 20 August 1988 and 17 December 1988.
48 *Drammens Tidende,* 21 November 1987.
49 Jan Åke Pettersson, *Odd Nerdrum* (Oslo: Dreyer, 1988).
50 Oscar Wilde, «Preface» to his *The Picture of Dorian Gray.*
51 Nerdrum, *Notater,* p. 47.
52 *Tique* 3 (1992), p. 38.
53 Michael Kvium, «Det intrigante maleri – Intervju med Odd Nerdrum» [The intriguing painting: an interview with Odd Nerdrum], *Fredag* (Copenhagen) 27 (1990), p. 37.
54 *Dagbladet,* 29 September 1990.
55 Conversation in Stavern, 25 February 1998.
56 *Natt & Dag* 6:2 (1990), p. 3.
57 Nerdrum, *Notater,* p. 88.
58 Ibid., p. 45.
59 *Dagbladet,* 3 August 1990.
60 Einar Jonsson (1863-1922). See, e.g., his *Morgengry* [Dawn] from 1897-1906, in which the outstretched arm, the fist, and the grotesque facial expression resemble Nerdrum's figure.
61 *Aftenposten,* 7 September 1990.

## THE SELF-REVEALER

1 Stig Andersen, «Narsissisme er selvforelskelse – om speilinger av jeg'et,» [Narcissism is being in love with oneself – reflections of the ego] in NRK TV's *Kultursjokket.*
2 Pettersson, «Odd Nerdrum: Evighetens synsvinkel,» p. 17.
3 Video recording from the student union in Bergen, 19 September 1991.
4 The issue of Nerdrum's statements of intent was also part of the discussion at the Bergen meeting. When Nerdrum had finished his presentation, his opponent, professor in the history of ideas at the University of Oslo, Trond Berg Eriksen, sharply criticized Nerdrum's statements: «I don't normally like to hear Nerdrum explain his art – what he has to say is either in the picture and therefore superfluous, or else it is not in the picture, and in that case he had better go all the way and become an author.» He also pointed to a tendency he had noticed for Nerdrum to include explanations in his pictures: «The element of over-transparency irritates, for it presupposes that the viewer is myopic or impaired. What might be called the work's immanent truth may also be endangered by extraneous commentary and by a sort of educational urge that won't rest until the entire class has grasped the curriculum. This inclination towards over-transparency creates an artlessness, because the creator hovers over his audience, asking, «Do you get it now? Do you get it now?»
   Nerdrum, who had just confessed to being a blatant self-revealer in his art, parried: «When it comes to transparency, I don't believe I can ever be clear enough. It depends on the artist himself – if he is intriguing as a thinking human being … In order to articulate something – to find it, to see it, to make it public – it has to be transparent and at the same time informative… In speaking publicly about my pictures, I have mostly tried to avoid any form of interpretation of my work. This is due to my feeling that what I make is transparent enough, so there is no need to say anything about it.» Later in the debate he also stated that chance played no part on the intentional level when making the pictures: «All of my ideas for pictures are carefully thought out ahead of time. It has all been there – much better and more wonderful than what I was able to paint. Everything is within me beforehand; it only has to be brought out and turned into a decent copy of what I already had inside.»
5 Nerdrum, *Notater,* p. 42.
6 Jan-Erik Ebbestad Hansen interviewed in *Vi menn* 11 (1995), p. 2. The story is repeated in his *Fenomenet Nerdrum,* p. 153.
7 Nerdrum, *Notater,* p. 98.
8 Ibid., p. 21.
9 Ibid., pp. 126, 56.
10 Odd Nerdrum, «Tvillingsjeler» [Twin souls]. *Rembrandt - Ridderen med falken* [Rembrandt - Man with a falcon] (Bergen Art Museum, 1992), p. 9.
11 Fellow exhibitor was Børre Larsen, and it took place 5 September – 29 October 1992. This writer provided the text for the catalogue, published in *Terskel* 8 (1992).
12 *Dagbladet,* 23 July 1992.
13 *Dine penger* 5 (1992), p. 40.
14 Nerdrum, *Notater,* p. 68. His Anine model had now returned to the studio to pose for this painting.
15 *Aftenposten,* 1 November 1991.
16 Nerdrum, *Notater,* p. 118.
17 Ibid., p. 21.
18 Jan-Erik Ebbestad Hansen, «Odd Nerdrum og kritikken» *Samtiden* 2 (1990), p. 57. He toned down polemics in his *Odd Nerdrum: Paintings* (Oslo: Aschehoug, 1994). See his notes 23 and 43 on pages 67-68.
19 Nerdrum, *Notater,* pp. 55, 21.
20 Information about this possible connection came from Nerdrum's friend and former pupil Per Lundgren. In the early seventies Grimeland also used Nerdrum as a model for the figure of Cain, who horrified and repentant leans kneeling over his slain brother Abel and has his hand to his face in the same gesture.
21 Nerdrum, *Notater,* p. 63.
22 Before publishing, the editor of the journal, Trond Berg Eriksen, organized a public meeting where Ebbestad Hansen presented his critical views. Both Nerdrum and this writer were present, but none of us participated in the debate that followed.
23 Nerdrum, *Notater,* p. 122.
24 Ibid., p. 90.
25 *Aftenposten,* 9 December 1995.
26 Nerdrum, *Notater,* p. 45.
27 *Aftenposten,* 20 June 1988.
28 *Dagbladet,* 14 June 1996.
29 Even the American conceptual artist Joseph Kosuth, who exhibited in Oslo in the fall of 1995, made a pretty feeble attempt at stopping the two professorships. The minister of education had made a speech at the academy in which he argued in ten points that it was both natural and necessary that a publicly supported academy teach also figurative art at the highest level. Kosuth then penned his *Ten Other Points for Norway,* where he argued against the minister and for barring this type of art from an academy, because it was «populist» and not in line with the art of our own century. The fact that there were many young artists who wanted to learn figurative painting and sculpture to express themselves on an advanced level, was to him irrelevant. They were into the wrong kind of art. (See *UKS Forum,* 3 April 1995).
30 Some figurative painters also turned against the appointment of Nerdrum. Their spokesmen were Dag Hol (*Aftenposten* 12 June 1996), Vebjørn Sand, and Thorvald Lund-Hansen, as well as Terje Moe and Ulf Nilsen (*Dagbladet* 11 June 1996).
31 Editorial in *Dagbladet,* 18 June 1996. As remarkable as the content of this personal attack is the fact that there has so far not been a single public response to it.
32 Nerdrum, *Notater,* p. 33.
33 Ibid., p. 57.
34 Nerdrum himself refers to this incident in *Verdens Gang,* 20 April 1997. He probably did not have the smile of Zeuxis, said to have inspired Rembrandt in his last self-portrait, in mind here, but rather pure euphoria.
35 Taped conversation 30 March 1994.
36 Drammen kunstforening, May 1990.
37 Producer of the exhibition was Kunsthuset A/S by Bjørn Li, while this writer was the curator. It was scheduled to open at Blomqvist's in Oslo in April 1996, to move on to Millesgården in Stockholm a month later. Each artist was to participate with eight paintings.
38 His Norwegian colleague Patrick Huse had enough works available to join him on short notice.
39 Mariani's *Constellation of Leo* from 1980-81 was begun at the same time that Nerdrum finished *Refugees at Sea* and was nearly the same size.
40 Unpublished manuscript for a lecture tour of the U.S., 2-10 November 1988: New Jersey, San Francisco, and Madison, Wisconsin.
41 Nerdrum, *Notater,* p. 106.
42 The American art historian Richard Vine probably got it right when he described Nerdrum's pictures as «icons for agnostics» in the exhibition catalogue *Odd Nerdrum: the Drawings* (New Orleans: Museum of Art, 1994), p. 13.
43 Nerdrum, *Notater,* p. 13.
44 Taped conversation 25 January 1998.
45 Interview with Per Ståle Lønning, TV2, 9 March 1998.
46 *Verdens Gang,* 6 December 1997.
47 Taped conversation 10 April 1998, all of which was devoted to his kitsch concept. The discussion in this paragraph and the next is a summary of this conversation.
48 See Hermann Broch, *Kitsch og kunst* [Kitsch and art] (Oslo: Cappelen, 1992), and Milan Kundera, *The Unbearable Lightness of Being* (Boston: Houghton Mifflin, 1976).
49 Kundera, *The Unbearable Lightness of Being,* p. 248.
50 Recorded conversation, 10 April 1998.
51 Nerdrum, *Notater,* p. 100.

## NOTES TO DONALD KUSPIT

1 George Frankl, Civilisation: *Utopia and Tragedy, The Social History of the Unconscious,* vol 2 (London: Open Gate Press, 1990), p. 167-68
2 Ibid., p. 164-65
3 Robert J. Stoller, Perversion: *The Erotic Form of Hatred* (New York: Delta Books, 1975), p. 4

# ODD NERDRUM, PERVERSE HUMANIST

AFTERWORD BY DONALD KUSPIT

*While we cannot bear to be fully conscious of the disappoint-
ments and tragedies, the injuries to our narcissism which reality
causes us to suffer, they are revealed to us by the artist. His sensi-
tivity reflects experiences of which we have only been dimly aware, and he makes us face them. In our time, he shows us not only
the images of a machine-dominated world which pervades our
existence and confronts us with unimaginable dangers, but above
all the world's rejection of our humanity – our impotence and
sense of futility in a world which happens without us and takes
no notice of our judgments and aspirations. He shows us just
how dispensable we have become.*[1]

Looking at Odd Nerdrum's recent paintings, one is tempted
to say that he is a special sort of contradiction: an existential
humanist and morbid pervert in one. That is, his art affirms
the constancy of humanity in an inhuman world – in Frankl's
words, «the human self-image» in «a world in which the human being had disappeared»[2] – but it does so in a way that
reflects the perverse effect of the world's indifference on the
human self-image.

If, as Robert Stoller writes, perversion is «the erotic form
of hatred...a fantasy... primarily motivated by hostility» that

"portray[s] itself as an act of risk-taking,"[3] then Nerdrum's
risky figures embody the world's cruel indifference in their
crippled flesh, even as their bodies are erotically excited by
that cruelty. It is as though being emotionally crippled –
Nerdrum translates it into physical crippling – makes one
more sensual than one would otherwise be. Perversely, his
figures are aroused by their own ruined state, however much
their arousal confirms their self-hatred, an ironic version of
the world's hatred.

The desert that pervades Nerdrum's pictures symbolizes
the world's hostile indifference – the destructive abandon-
ment of human being to the nothingness – and Nerdrum's
figures are often reduced to nothing but their flesh, that is,
the bare minimum of existence. They are as naked as the day
they were born, yet about to die, or haunted by death. Often
missing one or more limbs, their bodies are already on the
verge of disappearing forever: no vision of resurrection in
Nerdrum's desert, only sickness unto absolute death. Yet
however severely injured by the world – Nerdrum's figures are
irreparably damaged – and however much their narcissistic
injury is visible in their flesh, they experience it as sensually
gratifying – a masochistic triumph over the sadistic world.
After all, they have to find pleasure somewhere: Nerdrum's
figures are existentially tortured, but they are forced to enjoy
it.

Thus, in a remarkable self-portrait, *Self-Portrait in Golden
Gown* – truly unique in the history of artists' self-portraits –
we see Nerdrum exhibiting an erection. It is a risky, hopeful
display, pointing skyward like the finger of John the Baptist
in Leonardo's strange painting of the saint. The erection is a
defiant act of self-assertion, yet there is something futile, even
self-defeating about it. It occurs in a dark vacuum – in the
solitude of the studio. The artist is aged and alone; his sexu-
ality can release itself only in the masturbation of his art. It
alone gives him real pleasure. Dressed in an archaic robe, as
gold as any king's – it reminds one of the theatrical robes that
Rembrandt, another King of Art, affected in many works,
even the most introspective, existential ones, as though the
wearing of the robe signalled that he had not completely lost
his mind to his art but still had a social identity and place –
Nerdrum lifts its cloth to show not only his erection but his
peculiarly unsullied yet heavy flesh. Like the erection, it is
about to sag: both are subject to the downward pull of gravity, which is the secret subject of the picture. The ironic secret of the picture is that the erection is about to collapse of
its own weight. After all, it cannot be held forever; it has to

give, like any flesh, and fall down, its seed spent, futilely or not. Perhaps more futilely than joyously, as the dark background, emblematic of mortality and entropy, suggests. And yet there is a certain joy in the light that falls on Nerdrum's belly and erection, picking them out of the darkness as though they were freshly born, in a way that seems to leave his aging face behind.

The very figure we look at undercuts the voyeurism of our look. The reclining odalisque in *Pissing Woman* may be voluptuous and seductive – her eyes invite us to enjoy the sight of her nakedness – but she has also lost all her limbs and is urinating. Indeed, the luridly luminous stream of her urine is surrounded by a halo, while her face is in darkness. It is a startling image, full of contradiction. One cannot help but recall the poem in which Jonathan Swift expresses his shock and incomprehension at the fact that his beloved, a beautiful woman, also defecated – a perverse contradiction for him, indeed, a Gordian knot that not even his poem could cut. The standing one-armed man who accompanies Nerdrum's perverse heroine – they are a truly odd couple, she passive and immobile on the barren ground, while he raises his one arm in an angry gesture – adds to the contradiction, making it all the more unresolvable and terrifying. He is hardly the sexual companion she may desire – she seems to prefer some person looking at the picture, as the direction of her glance suggests – yet they are emotionally compatible, for together they form a single state of misery.

Another oddly complementary naked couple appears in *Old Man with a Dead Maiden.* The beautiful young woman is stretched out on an animal skin, while the ugly, old and somewhat demented man sits up, his red cloak absurdly flowing behind him, his sword – symbolically unused in its scab-

bard – beside him. She is in fact dead, and he all but dead. They ironically represent two different stages of life and in different states of mind, but like all opposites they stay together, however much they can never be reconciled, not by sexual intimacy nor any other human exchange. Nerdrum pictures human beings and human relationships in all their unfathomable intimacy – a compound of absurdity and sterility, as fated and doomed as the bleak world they inhabit.

Nerdrum's three paintings are existential allegories. They epitomize his art, which is a peculiarly medieval psychomachia – even a contemporary version of miracle play – that deals with the conflict between the life-instincts and the death-instincts, subtly evident in the body, and taking their toll on it. The very grain of Nerdrum's pictures is fraught with the gnostic battle between biophilia and necrophilia, as his tenebrism indicates. He has in fact revitalized, even quintessentialized, what has become an Old Master cliché – the subtle oscillation and tension between light and dark that structures emotional life – showing that nothing in art is obsolete, so long as it can still be put to human use. Showing that Old Master methods are still fresh and meaningful is Nerdrum's way of indicating that however much human beings are subject to the terror of annihilation anxiety, whether for individual or social reasons, the consummate artistry with which their suffering can be represented triumphs over it. Nerdrum's human beings endure, however injured by the inhumanity of the world and their own inadequacy, just as his art will endure, however much it perversely drops us into the abyss of existence.

New York, May 1998
*Donald Kuspit*

# LIST OF WORKS

*The medium is oil on canvas unless otherwise specified. Dimensions are given in inches: height x width.*

1.  *A Father Finding His Son*, 1993. 63 x 63.
2.  *The Seabird*, 1978. Oil on wood. 10 ½ x 14 ½.
3.  *Old People and Children by the Sea*, 1978. Oil on wood. 10 ¼ x 17 ¼.
4.  *Amputation*, 1968–1974. 76 ¾ x 101 ½.
5.  *Hermaphrodite*, 1965–1981. 57 ½ x 39 ½.
6.  *Self-Portrait with Hat*, 1979. 31 ½ x 30 ¾.
7.  *The Murder of Andreas Baader*, 1977–78. 130 x 106 ¼. Astrup Fearnley Museum of Modern Art
8.  *Back*, 1979. 86 ½ x 63.
9.  *Refugees at Sea*, 1979–80. 132 ¾ x 200 ¾. Hessisches Landesmuseum, Darmstadt.
10. *Self-Portrait in the Evening Sun*, 1977–79. 33 ¼ x 27 ¼.
11. *Twilight*, 1981. 77 ½ x 102 ½.
12. *White Brick*, 1984. 16 ½ x 21 ¾. Walker Art Center, Minneapolis.
13. *Dentures*, 1983. 12 ¼ x 15 ½.
14. *The Baby*, 1982–1995. 22 ¾ x 33 ½.
15. *Portrait of a Child*, 1982. 63 x 44.
16. *Sigmund in Red Coat*, 1983–1995. 57 ½ x 43 ¾.
17. *Portrait of a Girl*, 1985–1995. 53 x 47 ½.
18. *Isola*, 1984–1995. 105 ½ x 68.
19. *Summer Day*, 1982. 59 x 88 ½.
20. *Man with Headband*, 1984–1994. 59 x 88 ½.
21. *Early Morning*, 1984. 61 x 94 ½.
22. *The Evening Star*, 1984. 35 ½ x 43 ¼.
23. *Man in Abandoned Landscape*, 1968–1984. 48 x 65.
24. *Iron Law*, 1983–84. 82 ¾. x 107.
25. *The Mother*, 1985–1994. 59 ½ x 69.
26. *The Transfiguration*, 1984–1997. 69 ¼ x 98 ¾.
27. *The Ultimate Sight*, 1985–92. 46 ½ x 57 ½.
28. *Portrait of Arild Haaland*, 1984. 37 x 32.
29. *The One-Armed Aviator*, 1987. 45 ½ x 35 ¼.
30. *The Night Guard*, 1986–1998. 80 ¾ x 98 ½.
31. *Revier*, 1986–1998. 51 ½ x 63.
32. *Return of the Sun*, 1986–1995. 41 ¾ x 63 ½.
33. *Isola*, 1987. 25 ½ x 32 ¼.
34. *The Memory Hall*, 1985. 45 x 47.
35. *The Water Protectors*, 1985–1993. 98 ½ x 80 ¾.
36. *The Cloud*, 1985–1993. 48 ½ x 54 ½.
37. *Man with a Leather Helmet*, 1985–1995. 34 ¼ x 28 ¾.
38. *Man with Seeds*, 1986–1992. 52 ½ x 43 ¾.
39. *Sleeping Courier*, 1986–1996. 66 x 76 ¾.
40. *Armed Woman*, 1986–1993. 33 x 28.
41. *Sole Morte*, 1987–1993. 69 ¾ x 77 ½.
42. *The Black Cloud*, 1986. 62 ½ x 76 ¾.
43. *Sleeping Twins*, 1987. 98 x 96 ½. Museum of Contemporary Art, San Diego, California.
44. *Woman with Milk*, 1988–1993. 92 ½ x 82 ¾.
45. *The Seed Protectors*, 1987–1996. 63 ¾ x 76 ¾.
46. *Man against Open Sky*, 1988–1990. 43 ¾ x 46.
47. *The Storyteller*, 1988. 76 x 114 ¼.
48. *The Singers*, 1987–88. 76 x 97.
49. *Man in Sunset*, 1989. 43 ½ x 37 ½.
50. *Dawn*, 1990. 76 ½ x 112.
51. *Wanderer Imitating a Cloud*, 1990. 90 ¼ x 77 ¾. Astrup Fearnley Museum of Modern Art, Oslo.
52. *Woman with a Door Handle*, 1990. 45 ¼ x 53.
53. *Idiota*, 1990. 68 x 65 ¼.
54. *Three Namegivers*, 1990. 89 x 81 ½.
55. *Two Men Guiding One Man*, 1990. 72 ¾ x 80 ¾.

56. *One Storysinger*, 1990. 54 x 68.
57. *Contra Natura*, 1990. 59 x 79.
58. *Twins with Knives*, 1991. 43 ¼ x 46.
59. *Man Bitten by a Snake*, 1992. 93 x 105 ¼. Frye Museum of Art, Seattle, Washington.
60. *Sleeping Couple*, 1991. 43 ¼ x 39 ½.
61. *Self-Portrait with Closed Eyes*, 1991. 27 ½ x 31 ½.
62. *Blind Wanderer*, 1992. 94 ¾ x 108 ¾.
63. *Boy with Twig*, 1992. 35 ½ x 29 ½.
64. *Man with Shield and Stone*, 1992. 53 x 39 ½.
65. *Man with Torch*, 1992. 35 ½ x 29 ½.
66. *Five Persons around a Water Hole*, 1992. 111 x 139 ¾. New Orleans Museum of Art, Louisiana.
67. *Hermaphrodite*, 1992–96. 80 ¾ x 83.
68. *The Red Cape*, 1992. 59 ½ x 79 ¼.
69. *Man with Catfish*, 1992. 72 ¼ x 82 ¼.
70. *Woman with Fish*, 1994. 65 x 61.
71. *Self-Portrait with Eyes Half Closed*, 1991–93. 43 ¼ x 39 ½. The Metropolitan Museum of Art, New York.
72. *Man with a Horse's Head*, 1993. 58 ½ x 61 ½. Bergen Art Museum.
73. *Dying Couple*, 1993. 96 ¾ x 107 ¾. Göteborg Konstmuseum, Gothenburg, Sweden.
74. *Woman Killing Injured Man*, 1994. 78 ¾ x 114 ¼. Astrup Fearnley Museum of Modern Art, Oslo.
75. *A Pear*, 1990. 14 ½ x 17.
76. *Bread*, 1991. 27 ½ x 25 ½.
77. *Turid*, 1992. 17 ¾ x 13 ¾.
78. *Self-Portrait at Ystaas*, 1992. 17 ¾ x 13 ¾.
79. *Newborn*, 1993. 27 ½ x 30 ¼.
80. *Girl with Butterfly*, 1994. 72 ¾ x 17 ¾.
81. *Man with a Woman's Head*, 1994. 72 ¾ x 57.
82. *Dr. Kagul*, 1994. 35 ½ x 31 ½.
83. *Sigmund*, 1994. 31 ½ x 27 ½.
84. *Five Namegivers*, 1994. 74 ¾ x 65.
85. *Three Men at Dawn*, 1996. 73 ¼ x 61.
86–90. *Studies of Anne Sofie*, 1994 –95. 15 ¾ x 13 ¾.
91. *Baby in Deserted Landscape*, 1995–96. 35 ½ x 38 ¼.
92. *The Lifesaver*, 1995–96. 59 x 45 ¼.
93. *Barter*, 1995–96. 71 x 82 ¾.
94. *Frontal Self-Portrait*, 1994–95. 29 ½ x 23 ¾.
95. *Unarmed Man*, 1995. 72 x 66.
96. *Buried Alive*, 1995–96. 43 ¼ x 45 ¼.
97. *Self-Portrait in Armor*, 1995–96. 39 x 33 ¾.
98. *Stripper*, 1996. 81 x 101 ¼.
99. *Hepatitis*, 1996–97. 80 x 75 ½.
100. *Dancer with Snake*, 1996. 68 x 70.
101. *Boy with Icon*, 1996. 47 x 40 ½.
102. *The Nightjumper*, 1996. 67 ¾ x 67 ¾.
103. *Initiation*, 1997. 81 ½ x 104.
104. *Man with Long Hair*, 1997. 67 x 43 ¼.
105. *Old Man with Dead Maiden*, 1997. 81 ½ x 98 ¾.
106. *Pissing Woman*, 1997–98. 80 ¾ x 99 ¼.
107. *Woman Resting on a Rock*, 1997. 59 x 59.
108. *Mother with Child*, 1997. 27 ½ x 39 ¼.
109. *Blue Self-Portrait*, 1997. 43 x 37 ¾.
110. *Self-Portrait in a Golden Gown*, 1997–98. 73 ¾ x 56 ¾.
111. *Twins*, 1998. 74 ¾ x 100 ¾.
112. *Night–Light*, 1981–1998. 35 x 30.
113. *Self–Portrait in Profile*, 1998. 33 ½ x 30 ½.

# CHRONOLOGY

## SOLO EXHIBITIONS:

| | |
|---|---|
| 1999 | Kunsthal Rotterdam, The Netherlands |
| 1998 | Astrup Fearnley Museum of Modern Art, Oslo |
| 1997 | Frye Art Museum, Seattle, WA |
| | Forum Gallery, New York, NY |
| 1996 | Cleveland Center for the Contemporary Arts, OH |
| | Museum of Contemporary Art, Downtown, |
| | San Diego, CA |
| | Millesgården, Stockholm (with Patrick Huse) |
| 1995 | The Arkansas Arts Center, Little Rock, AK |
| | The University of Iowa Museum of Art, |
| | Iowa City, IA |
| | The Patrick & Beatrice Haggerty Museum of Art, |
| | Marquette University, Milwaukee, WI |
| | Joslyn Art Center, Omaha, NE |
| | Pittsburgh Center for the Arts, PA |
| | Forum Gallery, New York, NY |
| 1994 | New Orleans Museum of Art, LA |
| | Galerie Gerald Piltzer, Paris |
| | Ingrid Raab Galerie, Berlin |
| | Galleri Unique, Eidsvoll, Norway |
| 1992 | Bergen Art Museum, Norway |
| | Museum of Contemporary Art, Oslo (with Børre Larsen) |
| | Jan Baum Gallery, Los Angeles, CA |
| | Edward Thorp Gallery, New York, NY |
| 1991 | Gothenburg Art Museum, Sweden |
| | Perimeter Gallery, Chicago, IL |
| | Lemberg Gallery, Birmingham, MI |
| 1990 | Ingrid Raab Galerie, Berlin |
| 1989 | The Nelson-Atkins Museum of Art, Kansas City, MO |
| 1988 | University Art Museum, California State University, |
| | Long Beach, CA |
| | The Museum of Contemporary Art, Chicago, IL |
| | Madison Art Center, Madison, WI |
| | Edward Thorp Gallery, New York, NY |
| 1987 | Drammen kunstforening, Norway |
| 1986 | Wang kunsthandel, Oslo |
| | Germans Van Eck Gallery, New York, NY |
| 1985 | Delaware Art Museum, Wilmington, DE |
| 1984–1993 | Martina Hamilton Gallery, New York, NY |
| 1983 | Gallery Bellman, New York, NY (with Per Ung) |
| 1982 | The Bedford Way Gallery, London |
| 1977, –79, –83 | Galleri Tanum, Oslo |
| 1972 | Galleri 27, Oslo |
| 1967, –70, –73, –76, –80, –84 | Kunstnerforbundet, Oslo |

## PUBLIC COLLECTIONS:

Arkansas Arts Center, Little Rock, AK
Arnot Art Museum, Elmira, NY
Astrup Fearnley Museum of Modern Art, Oslo
Bergen Art Museum, Norway
Drammen kunstforening, Norway
Fort Lauderdale Museum of Art, Fort Lauderdale, FL
Frye Art Museum, Seattle, WA
Gothenburg Art Museum, Sweden
Hessisches Landesmuseum, Darmstadt, Germany
Hirschhorn Museum & Sculpture Garden, Smithsonian Institution,
    Washington, DC
Metropolitan Museum of Art, New York, NY
Milwaukee Museum of Art, Milwaukee, WI
National Museum of Contemporary Art, Oslo
Museum of Modern Art, New York, NY
National Gallery, Oslo
New Orleans Museum of Art, New Orleans, LA
Norwegian Art Council, Oslo
City of Oslo Art Collections
Portland Art Museum, Portland, OR
Rhode Island School of Design, Museum of Art, Providence, RI
San Diego Museum of Contemporary Art, La Jolla, CA
Trondheim Art Museum, Norway
University of Arizona, Museum of Art, Tucson, AZ
University of Iowa, Museum of Art, Iowa City, IA
Walker Art Center, Minneapolis, MN
City of Århus Art Collections, Denmark

# BIBLIOGRAPHY

Andersen, Stig: "Odd Nerdrum: Raving Mad or Brilliant?" *Siksi – Nordic Art Review*, January 1991, p. 34-42

Anderson, Alexandra: "The Story Teller", *Smart Magazine*, March–April 1989, p.62-63

Arndtzén, Mårten: "The Nerdrum Posse", *Siksi – Nordic Art Review*, April 1996, p. 17

Baker, Kenneth: "Art About the Art World", *San Francisco Cronicle*, 21. September 1986, p.12

Bass, Ruth: "Realism: When a Rose is a Rose", *ARTnews*, February 1996, p. 93-94

Berland, Dinah: "Neo-Classicism for a Nuclear Age", *Sunday Press Telegram*, 22. March 1988

Bjørke, Lars: "Kjærlighet uten helter", *Morgenbladet*, 3. September 1992

Blehr, Karin: "Holdepunkter?" *Vi ser på kunst*, Oslo, 3/1992
 - : "Bedrag og behag", *Kunst og Kultur*, 3/1983, p. 146–156

Brenson, Michael: "Odd Nerdrum", *The New York Times*, 11. November 1988, p. C24

Brun, Hans-Jakob: "Maleriet 1940-1980", in Knut Berg (ed.): *Norges Kunsthistorie*, volume 7, Oslo 1983, p. 191-195
 - :"Etterkrigstid" and "De siste ti år", in Knut Berg (ed.): *Norges Malerkunst*, volume 2, Drammen 1993, p. 296-302 and 356

Cone, Michele: "Odd Nerdrum", *Flash Art*, October–November 1986, p. 76

Cooper, James F.: "Odd Nerdrum: Intriguing Art, Unique Vision", *New York City Tribune*, 23. May 1986, p. 12
 - : "Nerdrums Drawings Reflect Inner Vision", *New York City Tribune*, 5. April 1985, p. 5B

Daussy, Frédéric (ed.): *Odd Nerdrum*, exhibition catalogue, La Galerie Gerald Pilzer, Paris 1994

Daxland, John: "Isolated Moments in Time", *New York Daily News*, 11. November 1988, p. 15

Donohue, Marlena: "Odd Nerdrum Paintings Bring Past to Present", *Los Angeles Times*, 26. April 1988

Egeland, Erik: "Odd Nerdrum i Kunstnerforbundet", *Aftenposten*, 13. November 1988

Engh, Audun: "Odd Nerdrum: Jeg tror på åndskapitalisme", Interview *Gateavisa* nr. 2/85, Oslo

Flor, Harald: "Nerdrum-Geriljaen", *Dagbladet*, 6. February 1986
 - : "Nerdrum med Nyanser", *Dagbladet*, 1. December 1987
 - : "Nerdrums beste", *Dagbladet*, 3. September 1990
 - : "Undergangssyner", *Dagbladet*, 20. May 1992
 - : "To sjeler og en tanke", *Dagbladet*, 5. September 1992
 - : "Nerdrums blodige kjønnskamp", *Dagbladet*, 5. februar 1995

Fox, Catherine: "Apocalyptic Visions Outside The Mainstream", *The Atlanta Journal/The Atlanta Constitution*, 30. July 1993, p. C3

Fox, Howard: "The Dream Disturbed", *Odd Nerdrum*, The University Art Museum, California State University, Long Beach, CA, 1988
 - : "The Limits of Art", *Avant-garde in the Eighties*, Los Angeles County Museum of Art, 1987, p. 96-97

Glueck, Grace: "When Today's Artists Raid the Past", *The New York Times*, 21. juli 1985, section 2, p. H29, 31

Giuliano, Charles: "Get Real", *The Improper Bostonian*, 13. November 1993, p. 19

Grimeland, Joseph: "*Odd Nerdrum. Kulltegninger*, Oslo 1978
 - : "Fenomenet Nerdrum", in Haaland, Arild (ed.): *Odd Nerdrum. Bilder*, Oslo 1983

Grøtvedt, Paul: "Nerdrum. Spørsmål om liv og død", *Morgenbladet*, 6. November 1984
 - : "Voldens totale herredømme", *Morgenbladet*, 4. February 1986
 - : "Bilder uten håp", *Morgenbladet*, 10. desember 1987
 - : "Ubehaget i sivilisasjonen", *Samtiden*, nr. 2 1990
 - : "Den mest toneangivende", *Aftenposten*, 2. December 1990

Hauge, Øystein: "Siste dagers hellige dåre", *Bergens Tidende*, 30. March 1996

Hansen,
 Jan-Erik Ebbestad: "Den nye Odd Nerdrum", *Aftenposten*, 12. August 1988
 - : "Odd Nerdrum og kritikken", *Samtiden*, nr. 2 1990, p.51-61
 - : Foreword in Odd Nerdrum: *Notater 1967-1992*, Oslo 1992  p. 7-11
 - : *Odd Nerdrum: Paintings*, Oslo 1995
 - : *Fenomenet Odd Nerdrum*, Oslo 1996

Heartney, Elizabeth: "Apocalyptic Visions, Arcadian Dreams", *ARTnews*, January 1986, p. 86-93

Henry, Gerrit: "Odd Nerdrum", *Art in America*, October 1986, p. 166-167

Hill, Shawn: "Mystery Tour", *Bay Windows*, 11. November 1993, p. 31

Hompland, Andreas: "Kunstnaren i rustning", *Dagbladet*, 20. July 1996, p. 3

Humphrey, David: "New York Fax", *Art Issues*, March 1993, p. 32-33

Hvistendal, Else: "Norwegian Artist Odd Nerdrum in New York Exhibit", *Norway Times*, 27. April, 1995, p. 5

Haaland, Arild: *Odd Nerdrum. Bilder*, Oslo 1983

Jarmusch, Ann: "Mythic & Mysterious, Nerdrum's Art Looks To The Past, Darkly", *San Diego Union Tribune*, 28. July 1996

Jencks, Charles: *Post-Modern Classicism – The New Classicism in Art and Architecture*, Academy Editions, London 1987, p. 39-40, 54

Kempe, Jessica: "En Rembrandt efter katastrofen", *Dagens Nyheter*, 19. May 1996

Kimmelman, Michael: "Odd Nerdrum", *The New York Times*, 26. May 1989

Kimball, Roger: "Odd Nerdrum: New Paintings", *London Publication* 1996
 - : "Disturbing Odd", *The Spectator*, 31. May 1997, p. 48

Kramer, Hilton: "How Long Will Curators Ignore The Great Odd Nerdrum?" *The New York Observer*, 22. May 1995, pp. 1, 21
 - : "Odd Nerdrum: A Maverick Sets Acts of Voilence in Alien Landscapes", *Art & Antiques,* January 1996, p. 86-88
 - : "Nerdrum, New Old Master, Takes on the Big Subjects", *The New York Observer*, 26. May 1997, p. 1 and 33
 - : "Shock Treatment: Pity and Poor Artist who Dares not Transgress", *Art & Antiques*, Summer 1997, p. 116-117
 - : "Odd Nerdrum: Paintings at the Forum Gallery", *The New Criterion*, June 1997, p. 56-57

Krisch, Monika: "Geschundene Menschen in karger Landschaft", *Volksblatt*, Berlin 9. December 1990, p. 14

Kushner, Robert: "Odd Nerdrum at Forum", *Art in America*, December 1995

Kuspit, Donald B:  "Odd Nerdrum:  The Aging of the Immediate",  *Arts Magazine*,  September 1984, p. 122-123
      - : "Odd Nerdrum: The Human Constant", i *Odd Nerdrum. Recent Paintings*, exhibition catalogue, New York 1986
      - : "Odd Nerdrum", *Artforum*, May 1987, p. 145
      - : "Old Master Existentialism" i Ebbestad Hansen: *Odd Nerdrum:  Paintings*,  Oslo 1995
      - : "Odd Nerdrum", *Artforum*, December 1997
Larson, Kay:  "Shrinking History", *New York Magazine*, 5. October 1987, p. 101-102
      - : "Odd Nerdrum", *New York Magazine*, 15. April 1985
Loge, Øistein:  *I det forbudte landskap,* catalogue, Henie-Onstad Kunstsenter, Høvikodden, 1996, p. 8-13
Meyer, Robert:  "Odd Nerdrum i New York", *Samtiden* 2/1990, p. 35-50
Miro, Marsha:  "Odd Nerdrum is the Ingmar Bergman of Canvas", *Detroit Free Press*, 27. November 1991
McManus, Michael:  "A Neoacademic Dream", *Artweek*, 23. April 1988
Moffet, Kenworth:  "Odd Nerdrum, Maitre ancien de notre temps", i Daussy (ed): *Odd Nerdrum*, Paris 1994
      - : "Painting like the Old Masters: Odd Nerdrum",  *The New Criterion*, 6/1989, p. 54-55
Morgenstern, George:  "Er maleriet impotent?", *Morgenbladet*, 8. October 1987
      - : "Odd Nerdrums nomader", *Arbeiderbladet*, 18. December 1987
      - : "Kampen om Historien", *Aftenposten*, 29. December 1988
      - : "Heldig kunstnerisk symbiose", *Aftenposten*, 5. September 1992
      - : "Tvil om tvillingsjeler", *Aftenposten*, 17. September 1992
Nerdrum, Odd:  " 'Det nye' og kunsten", *Aftenposten*, 29. April 1972, chronicle
      - : " 'Det rasjonelle' og kunsten", *Aftenposten*, 10. June 1972, chronicle
      - : *Havfuglen*, Oslo 1978 and 1997
      - : *Notater 1967-1992*, Oslo 1992
      - : "Tvillingsjeler" i Pettersson, Jan Åke: *Rembrandt-Ridderen med Falken*, catalogue.  Bergen Kunstmuseum, 1992, p. 8-9
Nerdrum, Odd/
 Naess, Arne:  "Det uttrykksløse", Interview *Flux*, Nr. 12, 1996/2, p. 22-29
Nordgren, Sune:  "Romanticism – Borderliners – Expressionism", i *Norwegian Art*, catalogue, Gothenburg Art Museum 1987 p. 60-62
Pettersson, Jan Åke:  "Odd Nerdrum: From the Eternal Point of View",  *Siksi – Nordic Art Review*, Helsinki nr. 1/87, p. 1 (interview)
      - : *Odd Nerdrum*, Oslo 1988
      - : "Twin Souls", *Terskel* nr. 8/1992, Museum of Contemporary Art, Oslo, p. 128-138
      - : "Odd Nerdrum: Isolasjon", in Svein Olav Hoff (ed.): *Kunst og  kommentar*, Asker 1992, p. 124-126
Poirier, Maurice:  "Odd Nerdrum", *ARTnews*, September 1985, p. 140–141
Ranc, Jacques:  "Odd Nerdrum", i Daussy (ed.): *Odd Nerdrum*, Paris 1994
Raynor, Vivien:  "A Return to Classicism in Ridgefield", *The New York Times*, 14. July 1985
Rheims, Maurice:  "L'aigle en son haut vol", i Daussy (ed.): *Odd Nerdrum*, Paris 1994
Russel, John:  "Odd Nerdrum", *The New York Times*, 16. May 1986
Serck, Peter:  "Fabelbilder i skumring", *Klassekampen*, 17. September 1992
Shearing, Graham:  "Odd Nerdrum Challenges & Shocks", *The Art Enthusiast*, 16. October 1995
Sherman, Mary:  "Exhibit of Narrative Art Shows Underbelly of Life", *The Boston Herald*, 5. November 1993
Spring, Justin:  "Odd Nerdrum", *Artforum*, nr. 8/1993, p. 94
Steihaug, Jon-Ove:  "Odd Nerdrum in Context",  *Siksi – Nordic Art Review*, Helsinki, 2/1993, p. 33–35
Stensman, Majlis:  "Om Rembrandt vore norrmann: Odd Nerdrum", *Månadsjornalen*, 2/1994, p. 64–71
Sterneborg, Anke:  "Verluste der modernen Zeit", *Der Tagesspiegel*, Berlin 13. desember 1990, p. 4
Storm Bjerke, Øivind: *I det forbudte landskap*, catalogue, Henie-Onstad Art Center, Høvikodden, 1996, p. 3–7
Strømberg, Ragnar:  "Måste hästar vara blå?", *Paletten*, Göteborg, 4/1991, p. 4–6
Søbye, Reinhardt:  "Nerdrum - mester eller rollespill?",  *Billedkunstneren*, 9-10/1991
Sørensen, Gunnar
 (a.o.):  *Norsk maleri på 70-tallet*, Oslo 1980, p. 22–26
Temin, Christine:  "Anxious Salon: The Naked and the Dread", *Living Arts – The Boston Globe*,  19. October 1993, p. 61, 65
Testerman,
 Margaretha:  "Odd Nerdrum", *Arts Magazine*, September 1985, p. 18
Thorkildsen, Åsmund: "Nerdrum på vei mot Toppen", *Drammens Tidende*, 6. February 1986
      - : "Menneskelig Ømhet og Tragedie", *Drammens Tidende*, 23. November 1987
      - : "Kunstnerisk Fylde og armod", *Terskel* nr. 3/1990, p. 162–168
Ustvedt, Øystein:  "Er ikke Odd Nerdrum samtidskunstner?", *Aftenposten*, 14. October 1992
      - : "Nerdrums tilbaketrukne verden", *Aftenposten*, 7. February 1995
Van Proyen, Mark:  "The Hieroglyphics of Ambivalence", *Artweek*, 4. October 1986
Vine, Richard:  "Nordic Anxieties", *Art in America*,  September 1990, p. 170–177
      - : "Mastery and Mystery: The Drawings of Odd Nerdrum", i Bullard: *Odd Nerdrum: The Drawings*, catalogue. New Orleans Museum of Art 1994
      - : "Odd Nerdrum: The Drawings", *Arts Quarterly*, New Orleans Museum of Art,  July/August/September 1994, p. 8-9
Volle, Wenche:  "Lys og lett Nerdrum", *Aftenposten*, 15. December 1997
Waddington, Chris:  "Odd Nerdrum: Tracing The Future of Art in Charcoal", *The Times-Lagniappe*, 2. September 1994, p. 14–15
Wiig, Einar:  "Fra mesterverk til kitsch", *Bergens Tidende*, 30. May 1992
Wivel, Michael:  "Et norsk fænomen", *Information*, 18. January 1977
Wright, David H.:  "Postmodern Art at the Modern Museum, *Berkeley Tri-City Post*,  1. October 1986

1998 © Aschehoug & Co.( W. Nygaard), Oslo
Translation: Inger Fluge Mæland and Jan Åke Pettersson
Editorial Direction: Tove Storsveen
Graphic Design: Anneli Skaar Graphic Design, Oslo
Reproductions: Litodesign by John Christian Sjølie, Oslo
Printing and Binding: Printer Portuguese
Printed in Portugal

ISBN 82-03-22272-2

*Copyright on works:* © *Odd Nerdrum/BONO 1998*

*This book has been published in conjunction with the exhibition* Odd Nerdrum: Paintings 1978 - 1998 *at Astrup Fearnley Museum of Modern Art, 09.25.1998 – 01.03.1999 (kat.nr.20), and at Kunsthal Rotterdam, 01.16. – 03.28.1999. Curator: Øystein Ustvedt.*

ILLUSTRATIONS:

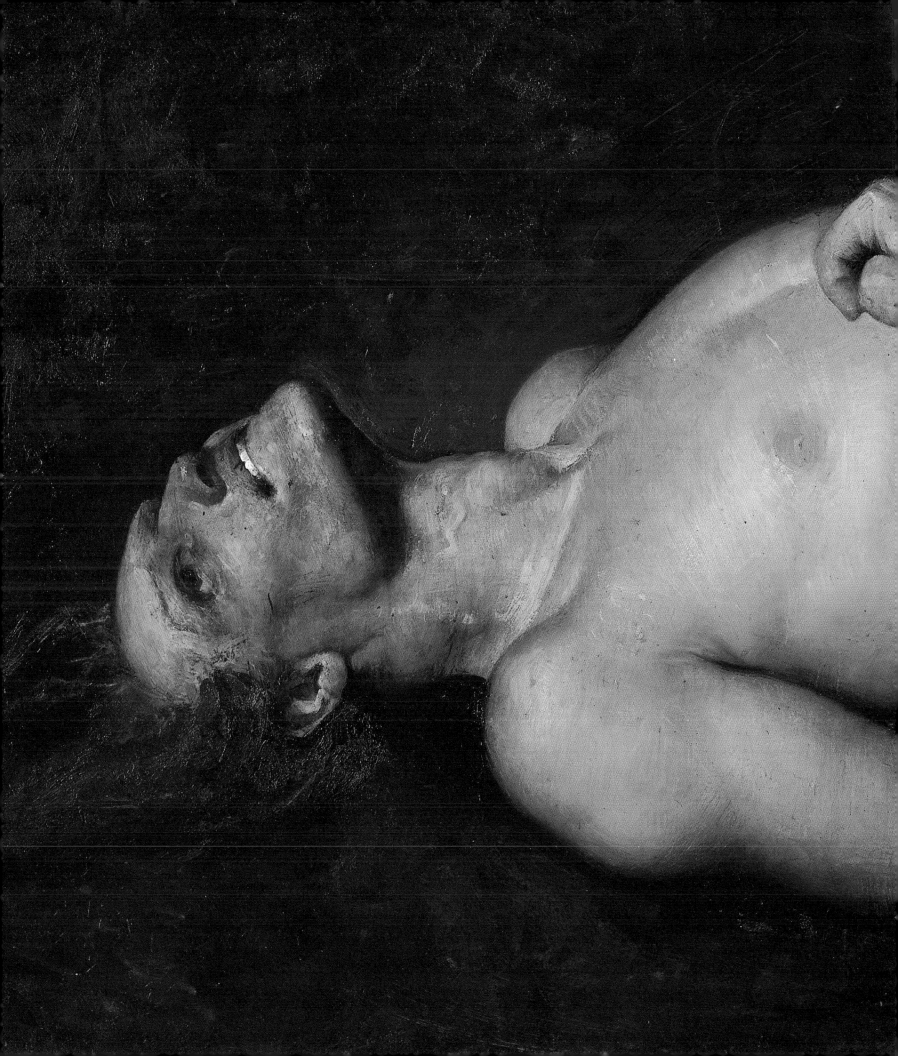

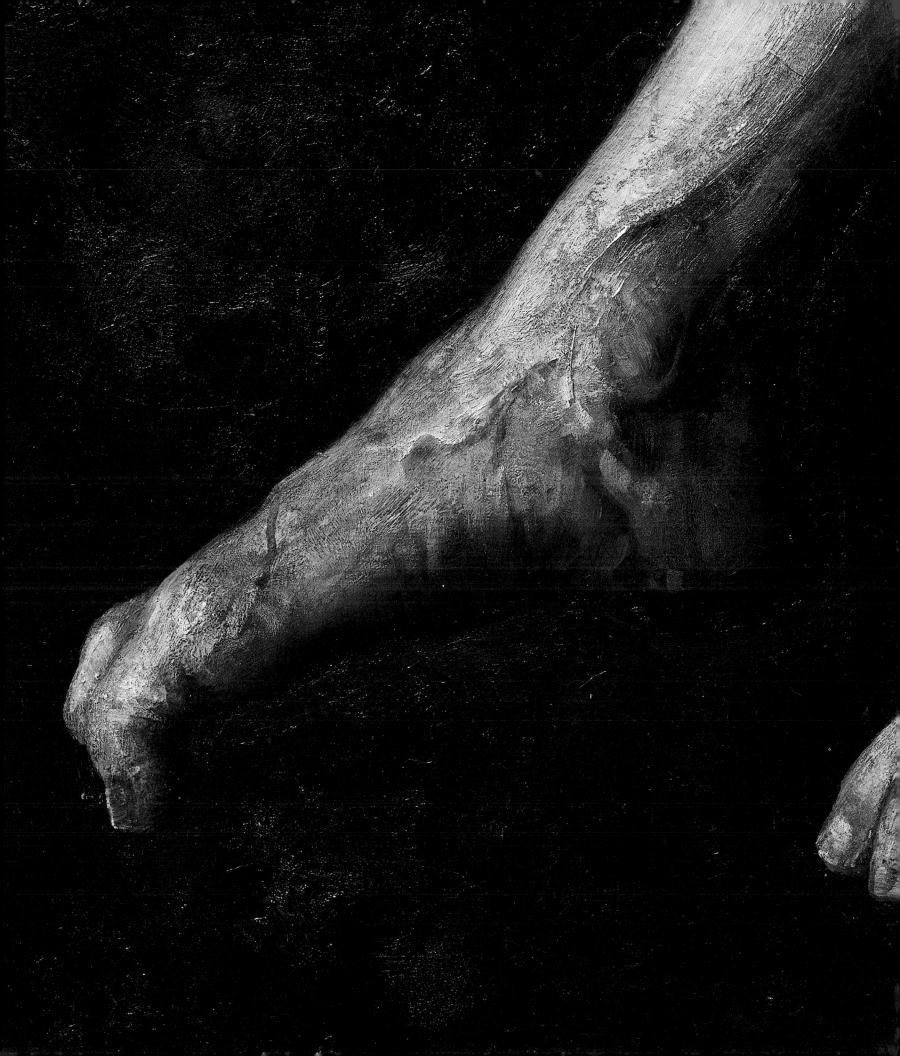

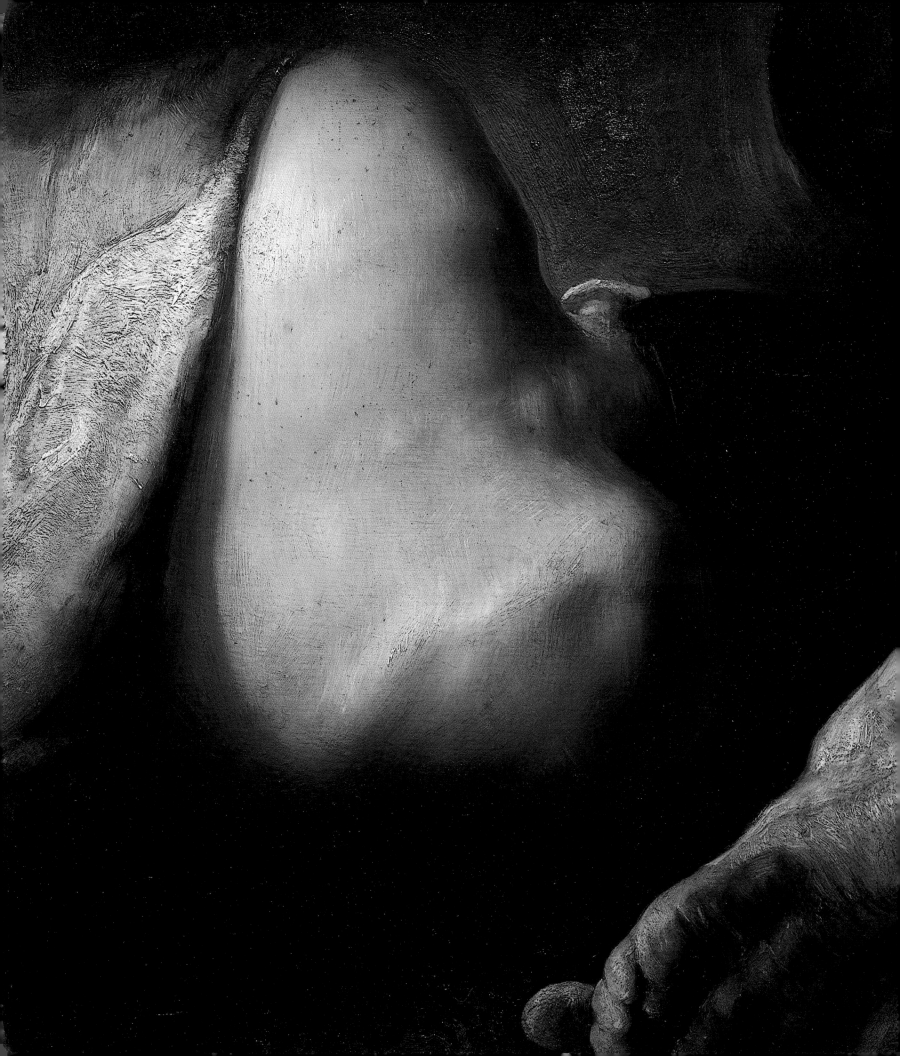